Magic from the Hilltops and Hollers

"The magic of Appalachia is the magic of the home and hearth, of the dirt and plants, of the mountain and river. Within these pages, you will find magic that is as authentic, timeless, and warm as a cup of tea steeped with intention or a quilt that holds a prayer in every stitch. *Magic from the Hilltops and Hollers* is a beautiful tribute that weaves the history, traditions, lore, and folkways of Appalachia with Leah's own lived experience and deep love for the region."

—Celeste Larsen, author of *Heal the Witch Wound*

"A beautiful ode to the magic found in the Appalachian region. Whether you're new to folk magic or looking to deepen your connection to it, *Magic from the Hilltops and Hollers* is a must-read. Leah's prose is immersive, weaving personal stories with ancestral wisdom and cultural nuance—her words don't just explain magic, they make you feel it. The book is practical, down-to-earth, and refreshingly unassuming with recipes, charms, and more to inspire your magic."

—Ivy Corvus, author of *Chaos Magic*

"Tender, spiritual, occasionally provocative, and always magical, *Magic from the Hilltops and Hollers* is a book that those invested in the world of living folklore will love and turn to over and over again."

—Cory Thomas Hutcheson, author of *New World Witchery: A Trove of North American Folk Magic*

"Having grown up in the mountains of western North Carolina and eastern Tennessee, I could feel the presence and influence of those areas throughout this resonant and powerful book—but you don't need to be from there to understand it. Engaging, warm, and nurturing, Leah's writing and mastery of Appalachian folk magic is as inviting as it is profound. For any person looking for a fully comprehensive, yet personal approach to folk magic, look no further."

—Anthony Perrotta, astrologer, stylist, poet, and designer;
IG: @ap_astrology

"Middleton's book is vibrant. Her voice paints the beauty and richness of not only Appalachian folk practice but the region itself through her experiences. She pays homage to the nature, the people, and the spirits of the Appalachians in a way that creates a mesmerizing manual for all those interested in the folk magic, medicine, plants, and people of the Appalachians."

—Frankie Castanea, a.k.a. Chaotic Witch Aunt

"A delightful collection of beliefs and lore celebrating Appalachia; it's a travelogue inviting readers to contend with the real history of those who lived and died and made magic within those ancient mountains. A compelling blend of memoir and grimoire that will have you seeking out Blue Ridge vistas on the horizon and hearing the distant cry of nightjars in your heart."

—Don Martin, author of *The Dabbler's Guide to Witchcraft*

MAGIC
FROM THE
HILLTOPS
& HOLLERS

Folk Witchery, Superstitions
& Healing Practices from Appalachia

LEAH MIDDLETON

FOREWORD BY **REBECCA BEYER**, AUTHOR OF *WILD WITCHCRAFT*

WEISER BOOKS

This edition first published in 2025 by Weiser Books, an imprint of
Red Wheel/Weiser, LLC
With offices at:
65 Parker Street, Suite 7
Newburyport, MA 01950
www.redwheelweiser.com

ISBN: 978-1-57863-880-2

Library of Congress Cataloging-in-Publication Data available upon request.

Cover and interior design by Sky Peck Design
Interior photos/images by iStock / Shutterstock
Typeset in Adobe Aldine

Printed in the United States of America
IBI
10 9 8 7 6 5 4 3 2 1

This physical representation of the region's magic wouldn't be without those who have taught and encouraged me along this path. A thank you to my old friend and first teacher, Jasmine, who introduced me to the early healing practices. A thank you to Shannon, a dear friend and teacher, who taught me how to listen closer and navigate the wooded pathways, and has always been there to remind me of my roots. A thank you to my Mamaw Nora's spirit, who has been holding my hand in this work. And lastly, a special thank you to those who embrace this region for all that it is and for furthering the narrative by sharing your voices. May we all continue to stitch our stories together for generations to come.

CONTENTS

6

A Tale Worth Telling: Exploring Southern Appalachian
Superstitions, Spirits, and Omens, 165

7

The Finished Binding, 201

Epilogue, 213

References, 215

FOREWORD

What is Appalachia? Is it a place? A feeling? A type of person? Perhaps it's something else entirely. Maybe it is both all of these things and none of these things. Writers have grappled with this idea since the late 1800s, when the notion that there was something both remarkable and different about the mountainous bioregion from roughly western Pennsylvania to northern Alabama was born.

I am both a researcher and practitioner of Appalachian folk magic and herbalism. After moving back to Appalachia in 2010 after a childhood being away from the mountains, I dedicated the last fifteen years to meeting the plants and beings of my region. I entered into the academic world of Appalachian studies and threw myself into learning the ethnobotany of our home. I have spent thousands of hours trying to understand what Appalachia is, and why it is special. Here in this book, Leah has taken up the same mantle, one I hold so dear to my heart. There is something in this land that calls many of us home, and something that those of us who move away may always think on with some measure of longing. But what is it?

She, born and raised in the place I now call home, has been called away on her life's journey to the western side of this huge landmass of Turtle Island. I know both of us could not have learned these ways without our teachers: people in our lives, books, and the land. We have both fallen under the spell of loving Appalachia and its folkways.

Born of her lived experience growing up in western North Carolina, Leah has given us a gift here with this book: a humble, honest look at the ways in which this region was born and her own place in it. Leah shows us a path to begin or continue practicing Appalachian folk magic while adding to the curious conversation of what makes Appalachia. It is not just a lonely log cabin in the woods, but a rich tapestry of both mirth and woe woven together to build the practice we hold so dear. It is the truth behind the honest reflections on both the difficulties and the sweetness of being a part of this place.

This book begins with a history of Appalachia and all of its people, journeying through personal stories and practical advice about how to charm and protect oneself using the old ways that have come to form the grimoire of mountain spells. It meanders like a mountain branch through some of the foundational omens, superstitions, weather lore, and the like. Leah shows us that Appalachian folk magic is far from the ways of an imaginary place trapped out of time. In a world increasingly interested in Appalachia and its folkways, this book avoids the easy trap of both idealizing and demonizing this special place. *Magic from the Hilltops and Hollers* acknowledges the bloody history and difficult modern issues we face as a region, both geographically and culturally, while also appreciating those things which have come to define the wonder and preservation of old magics.

This is no easy feat in a world of AI-written mountain spell books and poorly researched pieces on Appalachia that still succumb to the polarized temptations of either scapegoating our home as the seat of ignorance in America or placing it on a folkloric pedestal. Most importantly, Leah acknowledges the contributions of Black and Indigenous Peoples to this body of lore, a practice that is imperative but often excluded when speaking of Appalachia. This is a place beyond just the Scots-Irish: It is a diverse folk culture born of colonization and enslavement, indentured servitude and extractive economies. It is this and so much more, as it is also born of triumphs, collective care, class consciousness, and perseverance.

I feel excited for you to be holding this in your hands if you have ever been curious about Appalachia and what makes it special. While there will never be a simple answer, this book stands as a valuable addition to the growing library of works on the lived experiences of Appalachians and how folk magic continues to be a valuable part of their cultural identity. I hope that after you read this you feel as in love with this land and its citizens, both human and more than human, as I do. Long live Appalachia!

—Rebecca Beyer, author of *Wild Witchcraft*

A NOTE TO THE READER

Southern Appalachian folk magic is the crossroads of many voices that call this region home. Folklorists and regional practitioners have had ongoing conversations that the traditions represented in Appalachia are not static relics of one single origin, but rather living practices shaped by adaption, exchange, and the diverse peoples who are present and who settled, immigrated to, and influenced the region. The evidence lies in the charms, healing practices, prayers, superstitions, and traditions when traveling down the mountain range. From the traditions carried by African, European, and Indigenous communities to charms born from their mingling, Appalachian folk magic is the manifestation of this exchange. Understanding this complex historic context of *why* and *how* allows us to be informative and mindful of our regional magic.

In my conversations with fellow practitioners on the topic of cultural appropriation, I feel a responsibility to encourage the reader to honor the voices of marginalized communities where the boundaries of closed spiritual traditions are established and communicated to avoid cultural appropriation and dilution. Appalachian folk magic can become a bridge to ancestral practices. There is an encouragement to acknowledge one's family story when exploring the plethora of spiritual practices, as many do coexist here. A folk practitioner will find their work to be most meaningful when rooted in their ancestral stories, relationship with the land, and personal spirit contracts, and in the case of being part of a closed practice, through the guidance of mentorship.

When investigating the traditions of our mountain home, we tread delicate waters, as the preservation of folkways has been mainly through word of mouth and revival of old documentation. The information on regional practices that was handed down may not always reflect their truest origins due to cultural erasure and assimilation. Some of these ways were distorted out of necessity and to fit into the context of time and place. If feeling lost in these rabbit holes of research, we may seek out our ancestors and the land to help guide us along the way. Or, perhaps, recognize the blank pages in Appalachia's story in remembrance of lost history.

The key is to approach the traditions of southern Appalachia with humility and a commitment to acknowledge the complex birth story of *how* and *why* this exchange between many hands occurred, giving credit where credit is due to prevent further erasure, and practice community care to positively preserve the many origins of influence that have come together to form Appalachian folk magic.

INTRODUCTION

No matter whereabouts you go, you will always be Appalachian.

As I slowly hiked up the sloping path, the grassy summit emerged into view. A wide-open field with a scene of rolling hills belonging to North Carolina or Tennessee from either direction. The walk was a steady incline with man-made stairs leading the way. It then leveled where many found spots to set up their overnight camping gear with a view. The hiking trail was known for sunset and sunrise chasing. Word got out about it and quickly became a popular spot for newcomers. I had made the intention to visit more frequently before overwhelming crowds took over. Finally reaching the top, I settled down on a flat grassy patch with my blanket to catch my breath. No matter how many times I hiked it, it seemed my lungs never strengthened.

I positioned myself to face the sweeping vista of the Blue Ridge Mountains ahead. A golden hue draped over the landscape as the Sun descended behind the ridgeline. The ground lit into a sea of golden earth. The faint Waxing Moon signaled that night was close. A painted bouquet of marigold and violet stretched across the sky. Perched atop this summit, I felt like I was sitting on buried treasure. Indeed, a sentiment shared by locals and visitors alike. The view was a familiar one, but I never allowed myself to take it for granted. Time moved slower up here.

I pressed my weight against the cool ground beneath. An anchor to something certain while experiencing uncertainty. The familiar mountains that I've come to learn and love outlined in the dusk shadows. All felt well from above, but I couldn't shake a nameless feeling in my chest weighing me down. A longing for something. Somewhere? My mind rambling to identify it. Sorrow? No. Nostalgia? Maybe. It felt deeper than words can express. A question too big to find a single answer. I should feel settled and confident in the arms of these mountains—*my* mountains. That is what they have taught me over the years. Yet, I felt untethered. Drifting. As if the place where I planted my roots might no longer be suitable soil. I was grasping for answers to find my place in this big world. Lost in the echo bouncing from mountain to mountain. *Where do I belong?*

Shortly after my birth along the Carolinas' state borders, my parents chased financial opportunities that led us to the Mississippi coastline. I have no recollection of our short time there except that I spoke my first words. They came out like an old Southern song with twists and twangs. By the time I was ready to begin school, we had left the Deep Southern coastline for the big city in the Pacific Northwest. My earliest childhood memories are held there. Riding my bike. Chasing after the ice cream truck. Catching the ferry boat over to the islands. While those memories have faded with time, I still vaguely recall the earliest joys.

When I began school, I remember attending classes separate from my classmates. Apparently, the way I spoke wasn't easy to understand, but I was young enough to relearn. My teachers provided additional lessons on enunciation in a "proper" manner—as if something were wrong with how I spoke. Even now, I've become hyperaware of how I talk. Not because I've retained the Southern drawl, but from a feeling of self-consciousness instilled at a young age. Now, I see it for what it was. The way I spoke needed to be "corrected." It has since felt more like a robbery. A sliver of my authenticity diminished to fit into a societal mold.

It wasn't long before we packed up again and set off for a cross-country move that would settle us back to familiar grounds. With my paternal grandparents just across the state border in South Carolina, my parents discovered a "sleepy mountain town" in western North Carolina. The town was in good ole Henderson County. A place conveniently close for family reunions but still far enough away to do our own thing. I didn't think we'd live there long. History proved that we were always on the move. Eight-year-old me thought that North Carolina was just another pit stop before our next grand adventure. Little did I know I'd spend the next two decades of my life there.

I have to admit, I didn't appreciate it at first. The feeling of settling down was unfamiliar. To fulfill the dream of moving again, I would create elaborate stories with my dolls moving to big cities. They always lived in tall-towered buildings and passed through large crowds in city streets. Young me wanted to be anywhere else. Not in a small town with no tall buildings. It felt quiet—almost *too* quiet. Nights looking out my window were spent dreaming that my parents would change their minds and we'd move again. But it never happened. Despite my longing to conspire The Great Escape, my mindset slowly shifted. We weren't going anywhere. That much became clearer as the months and years passed by. North Carolina was home, and I needed to get comfortable.

So, I spent time getting to know it. My brother and I had everything we needed growing up. A roof over our heads and food on our plates. We weren't lavish, and if we were struggling, my father never allowed it to be known. During sticky summers I went down to the backyard creek to feed faeries dandelions and make homes for turtles out of sticks and mud. I ambled along kudzu-covered pathways to an undeveloped back field, where I'd scavenge for treats left behind by nature. After getting dropped off by the school bus, I'd take long afternoon walks to a nearby park with an old swing set that overlooked the neighboring farm. When the fog was low and the Sun began to dip, the trees became fictional giants that stood between me and the French Broad River. If I had finished dinner early enough, I'd take my portable CD player and head to the park with whatever mix I'd illegally curated to stargaze in the open field. The lightning bugs orchestrated a show during the late summer evenings. Before I knew it, that park settled my young mind that this place was not all that bad.

By the time I was driving, I had become fully responsible for myself. In between work and school, I was exploring my hometown with my new-found freedom. Now the local trails and riversides became my new playground. Some days, when the weather was thawing from winter to spring, my friends and I would skip class to visit our favorite jam store that had every flavor under the Sun in the Highlands country. If it wasn't the Highlands, we'd wash away the stickiness from the humid air in Dupont State Forest's Fawn Lake. Upon returning to class the next day, our math teacher would ask where we went. We'd tell him honestly, and he'd follow it up with, "It was a beautiful day, I don't blame ya!"

Any spare time was filled with adventures cruising along the Blue Ridge Parkway, a scenic highway that begins in North Carolina and ends in Virginia. I'd pull over at a lookout to sit in the trunk of my Subaru and enjoy a sandwich. My eyes in awe of the curved edges from each mountain layer stacked on top of the other. Autumn was my favorite, as I'm sure you could imagine. The vibrancy of summer would be replaced with the sleepiness of winter, but not before the region put on a show for leaf-lookers (folks who weren't local to the area but visited every season to, well, look at the leaves). The landscape was painted by whatever divine architect you believe in with a delicate brush dipped in amber, goldenrod, and grape wine, an enchanting color palette unlike any other, displayed for all to take in, to gasp and stare in awe.

These most magical moments affirmed what *home* truly felt like when I closed my eyes. A fall tradition included grabbing my favorite flannel and heading to the apple orchards for cider and house-made doughnuts. We would spend entire days at neighboring farms, exploring between apple trees I grew up alongside. Every year, our small town hosted the Annual Apple Festival. I carefully selected Honeycrisp for my seasonal pies or to simply savor on my next hike. The early morning hours were spent exploring trails as the leaves began to cover the ground. *Crunch. Crunch.* The mountain air smelled of leftover campfires, and nostalgia made its acquaintance as I carved new memories with October sunsets behind me. I had begun to romanticize a place I had fought so hard against.

Soon enough, I had memorized the local trails like the back of my hand. I knew of all the backroad shortcuts, where to harvest berries, and how to scare off black bears should I ever need to. It was hard to admit sometimes, but I had fully immersed myself as part of these backwoods. They served as a groundwork for my identity. My familial roots had been present in these parts for generations. They spread beyond where I stood into eastern Kentucky, Tennessee, and beyond in West Virginia. My constant yearning for this ideal home had always been right in front of me. I was just too stubborn to admit it.

But this internal battle continued. One day, I'd be driving home from work, passing by the same views I always did, filled with immense gratitude that I get to call this place home. The next, I'd be researching cities on the opposite coast. I made a few attempts to move away and start anew, but the Blue Ridge Mountains were never quite ready to let me go. *Or was I not quite ready?* No matter what I did, I always felt like something kept calling me back. An invisible string that tugged at my heart. The truth is, I found solace as much as pain growing up in western North Carolina. There are memories both wholesome and upsetting carved into childhood tree trunks.

When talking with anyone from my hometown, you will get one of two narratives. On one end of the spectrum, some folks express their deep attachment to the place. They have no desire to live anywhere else, and the foundations have already been laid out for them. They value the quiet and the generations of their family history. Whatever their story may be, there is a sense of loyalty often referenced. On the other hand, some people idealize seeking out other places for new opportunities. Neither narrative is better than the other; I've grappled with both perspectives myself. Refusing to give up the natural beauty but also recognizing the rising economic hardship. It is a hard reality that strikes many locals and leads them to have to make some tough decisions. No matter which end of the spectrum someone might tend toward, the larger discussion requires some nuance. It is not the same story for everyone.

For me, I was chewed up and spit out of my hometown when the time came. Tumultuous years had followed to the point where I no longer felt like my mountain town wanted me around. I had hoped for some relief—prayer after prayer and spell after spell. I didn't expect to find the answer in the middle of a global pandemic, but there it was. The mountains that raised me were the same ones that pushed me away. They urged me to go, despite some reluctancy.

There are some nights I spend visiting familiar trails within the dream realm. Sometimes I'll catch myself praying for Spirit to give me a reason to return. Perhaps my story is meant to finish there, and I'll die among the blackberries with my ashes scattered in the river. I don't know what my future holds, but I know that my past growing up in those hills opened my eyes to not only home, but the magic that's alive, too. That's why you're reading this book after all, right?

Clutched tightly to my chest are the values forever carved in my heart and soul in everything that I do as a magical practitioner from Appalachia.

They aren't necessarily universal beliefs, but variations of them are common in Southern households. Perhaps some have a ring of familiarity, but the ones I was raised by are as follows:

Give thanks, always.
Respect your elders.
Be a good neighbor.

Southern Appalachians know a lot about hospitality and being a good neighbor. But it's never meant to be taken advantage of or mistaken for this "all-love-no-hate" motto. It's more like everyone has a place here and we welcome them as they are. Everyone is of equal nature. That's not to say it was peaceful all the time. History shows that relationships between families or neighbors would go south sometimes. There might be family feuds that percolate for generations, with names written on someone's shit list 'til the day they die. That's why it's best to remember these values just to err on the side of caution. You wouldn't want to accidentally get on the wrong side of someone's Mamaw or Papaw.

There is more than what meets the eye when people visit the southern region. These mountains are not for the faint of heart, that I can assure you. I've experienced the various tests that present themselves. They're often a reflection of what these rolling hills have witnessed themselves. Blood soaked deep in the earth, the roots of trees scarred from the extraction industries, and the fear of whether a cold is just a cold or something more without the work of a prayer. These experiences have profoundly influenced southern Appalachian folkways, emphasizing a resiliency and importance of persistent hope despite hardships. We take on the mindset of rolling with the punches. It results in us giving thanks in every circumstance, no matter how big or small the blessing. Yet, it's not all struggle here. That's not the only impression I want to leave you with. This place reflects the reality that two truths can coexist.

Let's make it clear here. When I speak about Southern culture, I'm referring to people like my father, who watched NASCAR on the weekends while he enjoyed a third cup of Folgers coffee and stripping green beans; my mother, who went to church every Sunday and spent her time making quilts for family members. My friend from Waynesville, who taught me how to identify a bear scent and showed me uncharted deep-wooded hiking trails. My high school friend, who hosted comforting potlucks and brought me herbal tea blends when I was sick. Late nights at Waffle House. Rooster wallpaper around the kitchen. *Country Living* magazines in the bathroom. This is the kind of southern Appalachia that I know. The one that opens its arms and embraces its neighbors.

Life along this mountain range varies from region to region as much as it does from family to family. Folkways and traditions are shared among neighbors, but for the most part, you'll see various methods depending on whether you're from one hill or another. Every family has a way of doing things, but nonetheless, for the same purpose. It shows that there is no one uniform Appalachian tradition. Rather, it is a tradition that celebrates many traditions under one umbrella. It'll be helpful to keep that in mind as we walk through this book together.

I am but a fragment of this diverse mountain range. My storyline is a speck on the map. It does not capture the entirety of southern Appalachia because I am but one person sharing my perspective as a practitioner, interweaving the folkways of my familial ancestors. It is my responsibility, I feel, to piece together the puzzle behind the "why" of the region's folk magic and witchery. I must dig deeper with little fear of getting my hands dirty. That is what this work asks of me. Perhaps visit unmarked graves. Maybe call upon ancestors whom I've never met in the flesh. Consult my neighbors of kin and visit old, craggy pathways. Hold space for those who may feel forgotten and listen to past-time stories.

It wasn't long before I became fixated on the quest to discover how my kin found themselves here. How did their lives change with the passing of time? What did they do to make ends meet? How did they pray? What spirits did they call to? If I had the opportunity to sit with my grandmothers in their kitchens or in their gardens, what skills would they teach me? What stories would my grandfathers share while sitting in their rocking chairs? I closed my eyes with the intent to reach into the deepest parts of my bones, asking for any sort of response, even from a different realm.

To understand the magic of southern Appalachia, one must peel back the layers of time, exploring the echoes of diverse traditions that have clung to the rocks like moss. Much like their ancestors, some individuals practiced a form of magic called anything but. Local healers and doctors of these hills and hollers did their work much of the time in spite of witchery. It was a way to protect their own and repel any signs of the devil. In these pages, we will wander down shadowy paths lined with rhododendrons, uncovering the corners where charms are whispered and prayers are spoken. We'll stand where the mundane and magical are blurred.

My upbringing and what I am familiar with is within the bounds of this southern region. How I am defining southern Appalachia is probably more appropriately referred to as "central southern," as it references several states: eastern Kentucky, eastern Tennessee, western North Carolina, western Virginia, and northern counties of South Carolina. In this district, there were various groups of immigrants, such as the English, Irish, Scots-Irish, French, and German, to name a few European diasporas. Indigenous Peoples, such as the Cherokee, Shawnee, Creek, and many more, resided in the southern mountains long before European arrival. The enslaved African peoples were forcibly brought here by the transatlantic trade that violently removed them from their homelands of western and central Africa. The colonization of southern Appalachia is just a sliver of the United States' birth story. Each of these cultures added their distinct identity to the region. With that, we have been gifted a rich and authentic culture of arts, music, food, stories, and magic that continues to be passed on today, uniquely labeled as *Appalachian*.

My goal is to make *our* mountains proud. Being from the southern Appalachian region has become a meaningful piece of my identity, my practice, and it informs the way I go about doing things. Whether it makes a whole lot of sense or not. I'm a curious mind inspired by digging deeper into the understanding of my ancestral roots and sharing my lived experience in these mountains. And I learn best through storytelling. Therefore, you'll find personal stories at the beginning of most chapters—like adding kindling to the campfire as we keep the oral tradition of storytelling alive. It's one of the ways we can continue to get to know each other. While writing this work, I had to remind myself that this isn't a scholarly or academic text; plenty of those are out there written by folks in much better positions to do so. This is more of a love letter to the mountain magic that survives here and an exploration of how it came to be, and how it can be applied today in a modern folk practice. Understanding the people's history is essential to understanding the foundations of any folk magical practice.

When sharing the superstitions, healing practices, and magic weaved intricately in the hillsides, I will do so with delicacy and respect. I also feel it is my responsibility to trace the origins of such traditions to the best of my abilities to prevent further erasure of their true identities. Let this be a representation of such aspiration, as well as ongoing work beyond this book. With that, you will find a section for further investigation of the resources I collected, knowing full well that more will emerge with time.

This book has been quite a journey for me, and I'm thrilled to have you be a part of it. You will find additional segments such as Mamaw's Book of Spells. For some practitioners, they've acquired much of what they know from their elders. My story is a bit different in that much of what I've learned has been from hands-on experience, inspired by folk recordings, and exchanged with fellow practitioners from my hometown. In my mind, if I were to gather material to pass along of my scribbled rituals and workings, it would be the ones that I share with you in this book.

During this writing process, I often found myself chasing a liminal rabbit when something piqued my interest. I followed these rabbit holes, completely consumed by a topic that would later serve a purpose. This inspired the segment Down the Rabbit Hole, where you may follow down into the rabbit hole with me.

These old woods were my childhood home, and yet here I sit across the country as I write this. Eventually, I did proceed with The Great Escape. There was a lot of grief that came with that decision. Uncertainty and fear. Writing this book is an ode to my Appalachian roots and ancestors, known and unknown, of blood and kin. The grandfathers who had dirt under their fingernails from farming in Kentucky. The grandmothers who bled while sewing their garments and quilts. The relatives who decided to take a leap of faith and pave a new path for themselves that may never be spoken about. The ones who passed away too young. The kind neighbors and compassionate friends who took me under their wings. The fellow practitioners and healers who showed me new methods. It is a work of veneration to keep their spirits alive. If you share similar roots to mine, or find yourself creating new ones, and have decided to embark on this path, may this book be a hand to welcome you *home*.

1

WELCOME HOME:
THE SOUTHERN HILLS OF APPALACHIA

When the humid summer air became a nuisance and the early morning hours were the only relief, I knew it was blackberry-picking season. Foraging for blackberries became a beloved annual tradition, but finding an untouched blackberry bush became a challenge as its popularity grew. Over the years, we had to venture higher and higher to find berries untouched by people and hungry black bears. I relied on my brother to know of a good spot. For personal enjoyment, he kept a record of less populated trails along the Blue Ridge Mountains. He came upon a trail abundant in bramble bushes, which he kept secret to ensure first dibs for a fine harvest.

We drove up the highway and headed south on the Blue Ridge Parkway. We passed by some of my favorite trailheads from previous berry-picking seasons. The rolling hills showed off their blue hues against the crystal clear skies. A sea of mountain waves. I rolled down my window to breathe in the fresh air, only to be smacked by summer's sweaty kiss.

We eventually pulled over onto a gravel road and eagerly gathered our tools: two empty, cleaned-out milk jugs—one for my brother and one for me; a flannel for the chill; and a machete in case the trail was overgrown. Following this narrow, barely recognizable path with its steep incline, we ascended what felt like miles—though, looking back, it was probably just my weak lungs making a rude statement.

As we gained altitude, the air blessed us with a cooler temperature than down in the valley. Clouds shaded us from the Sun, providing relief from the southern heat. The path led us through a blanket of trees with towering rhododendrons, and laurel bushes formed thick hedges around us. The ground was a carpet of wild ferns and moss. If you weren't careful, it'd be easy to get lost in the maze. My brother's voice interrupted my close observation: "Okay, here's the spot." We came into view of an open summit covered in blackberry bushes. With our empty milk jugs in hand, we got to foraging.

For each berry I plucked, I envisioned the tartness against my taste buds and noticed the purple juice that smeared my fingertips. After inspecting, I'd pop the occasional berry in my mouth. I'd go for another to add to my collection, glancing at the milk jug occasionally to vaguely measure. Ahead of me, my brother was deep in the bushes collecting his berries. The only way to find him in the distance was by spotting the tip of his red Marlboro hat and mustard T-shirt. My husband observed behind us, keeping an eye, ear, and nose open for signs of bears or other wildlife. He's not native to the region—heck, not even from this country—but he'd periodically comment on how at home he felt here, especially with the scene we had in view.

After collecting the berries we needed, we began our descent and drove home. Then we parted ways and retreated into the kitchen. Pies were first on my list. A flavor that never stops blessing our bellies. Jam was next. I am always delighted to share these creations with friends and family, each jam and pie being an intimate, delicious food offering from our home.

I didn't know that would be the last summer we'd go berry picking together at that spot. It's become a memory I hold near and dear to me. It's forever associated with the smell of baking with blackberries—a reminder of simple pleasures.

*A*ppalachia. Just the name tugs at your heartstrings. We won't dive into the debacle of pronunciation here. But I will say that where I come from, you will hear folks pronounce it as *APPL-ATCHA*. I've heard the running joke that if you mispronounce it you'd get an apple thrown at you. I can attest that that won't necessarily happen. You may just get an eyebrow raised.

The landscape of Appalachia consists of the world's oldest mountains that seem to go on for miles. The rugged terrain is a scene for the imagination. Granite faces cut into the cliffsides. Hilltop meadows veiled in a misty haze. Rows of trees interspersed with thickets and hedges, rivers carved through the valleys, and deep gorges with waterfalls putting on their best show. Long stretches of tall grass fields for the cattle to graze with background trees that experience the seasonal cycle of life. It is the perfect setting for picking apples and dancing with the devil.

The ears of distant historians, adventurers, artists, and naturalists had been drawn by curiosity, each seeking to capture the region's elusive spirit. Interested reporters and writers took on the quest to visit and record their personal experiences in hopes of unveiling what had been historically unknown. Yet, the truest understanding of Appalachia's soul can only be achieved through immersion. Only by being engulfed in its intricate landscape can you grasp all that it has to offer.

The landscape of southern Appalachia not only captured imagination but also influenced the early outside perceptions. The harsh beauty of the mountains formed a natural barrier from suburban areas. This boundary had long inspired speculative myths, leading to the creation of preconceptions about the mountain residents. The very mention of Appalachia often evokes an array of pastime fallacies. The term "hill billy," first recorded in the 19th century, exemplifies negative stereotypes that have long plagued Appalachian people. The first mention of the term appeared in the *Cincinnati Enquirer* on October 18, 1881:

THE TOWN TAKEN BY ROUGHS.

NICHOLASVILLE, October 17.—This has been Court-day, and a quiet one, until about dark, when ten or fifteen roughs, known locally as "Hill Billies," undertook to take the city.

Scholars argue that the term *hillbilly* has Scottish dialect roots. Nonetheless, it quickly became part of the American vernacular, adopted as a derogatory term for Appalachians. Appalachia was considered a secluded, past-time world inhabited by "other" people, untouched by modernism. Now, I'm happy to see that folks have begun reclaiming the term *hillbilly* from its offensive beginnings, using it as a point of local pride.

Despite the expansion of western states, the southern Appalachian region remained one of the most mysterious places. Lore traveled through the sea of hills into larger cities, which piqued a sense of curiosity for outsiders to document the unfamiliar residents, referring to them as *mountaineers*. Rumors suggested that Appalachians lived in a bygone era, clinging to their ancestral past and immune to the outside world. That's the thing about the unknown—it leaves room for the imagination to run wild.

The prevailing impression was that this "other" world was so backwooded that its people were peculiar, vicious, and full of outlaws. The difficulties of travel allowed for the majority to remain more secluded until roadways were formed through the rugged terrain. Before then, only those who were brave ventured into the area, and only a few sought to shed an honest light. Horace Kephart's *Our Southern Highlanders* was pivotal in the mountaineer's unmasking. Kephart immersed himself in a county that straddled the border between North Carolina and Tennessee—not far from my own origins. Having been an urban folk from St. Louis, his desire for a quieter life led him to the mountains of western North Carolina. Kephart took a special interest in surveying the Great Smokies, taking detailed notes of stories from neighboring residents. This published work would later paint a picture of the local *hillfolk*. His observation of the Great Smoky Mountains, the town's seasonal hardships, transportation challenges, and moonshining practices offered significant insights that combatted records that fueled misconceptions.

Historically speaking, media narratives have painted Appalachia as a monolithic region home solely to struggling white working-class families with strong conservative views. This portrayal attempts to erase the diverse stories of non-white individuals, queer communities, and those with radical views. This misconception has done a disservice in every realm—magical and otherwise. But Appalachians continue to dismantle this outdated image, shedding light on the region's reality and complexity, and crumbling these narratives at the seams. I invite folks to visit, shake our hands, and discover what we're all about for themselves.

DEFINING APPALACHIA

Before we explore the region's folk magic and witchery, we must first uncover the definition of southern Appalachia for a foundation to build upon. To do this we will briefly discuss the three ways it is defined: by nature, by the people, and by the government. In the following sections, we'll explore the ridgelines of Appalachia that led to natural state border-lines, pointing at monumental mountain peaks as well as the flora and fauna. Then, we'll explore the settlement history that makes up the multi-layered quilt. Lastly, we'll discuss how the government defines this region and its ongoing recovery efforts. Though this discussion may not have a primary focus on magic or witchery, it is the ground beneath our feet to build on.

By Nature

Nature itself shaped the division between northern and southern Appalachia over a long period of time. Repeated glaciations and ice sheets that once covered North America carved out the region's distinctive landscape, with its rolling hills and deep U-shaped valleys. These natural processes left a lasting imprint on the signature scenery, which continues to captivate visitors from all directions. People from other areas often tell me how they used to visit these mountains for family vacations to "get away from it all." The quietness found in hollows, the gentleness of backyard creeks, and lush green barriers make up the perfect landing spot for solitude.

Up north are the White Mountains of New Hampshire, the Green Mountains of Vermont, and the Adirondack Mountains of New York, just to name a few that belong to the northern Appalachian Mountain region. One summer, I visited a friend up in New Hampshire, where she took me hiking in the White Mountains. They were much grander than the ones I knew back home but still dressed in dense forests. It was odd to be so far away and yet still feel like I was on familiar ground. The hike she took me on in Flume Gorge followed a skinny, rocky trail along the mountain. It crossed over bridges that led to waterfalls flowing into the river below us. It felt like a territory belonging only to the local cryptids. Instead, we were intruding with other visitors who took the morning off to explore.

Further south into West Virginia and Pennsylvania, we're met with the Allegheny Mountains. This historically significant subrange played a crucial role in the growth of the transportation, steel, and timber industries during the Industrial Revolution, with the Baltimore and Ohio Railroad (BO) overcoming the terrain. This mountain subrange begins at the West Virginia–Virginia border and extends north into Pennsylvania. The Alleghenies are important mountain allies for northern Appalachian practitioners as they are soaked in local folklore.

We then come to what I'm most familiar with, my home mountains, the renowned Blue Ridge Mountains and the Great Smoky Mountains. These subranges serve as a natural border between western North Carolina and eastern Tennessee. They're also home to some of the largest peaks east of the Mississippi River and include the tallest mountain on the east coast. Mount Mitchell, or Attakulla, stands at 6,684 feet in Yancey County, North Carolina.

The day I finally explored the great mountain was shortly after the weather broke from an icy winter season. It had been on the hiking list for years, but I was always weary of exploring touristy trails. *Give me a trail that nobody knows and a chance to never be seen again—that's where I'll be!* We parked up and prepped the dog with hiking gear, grabbed our Nalgene water bottles, and began the Balsam Nature Trail, which was less than a mile. Piece of cake. All was well except . . . my shoes. One embarrassing thing about me is that I am notorious for never accurately being prepared. You'd think I'd learn, but I never do. Whenever the Sun is out, no matter what, I always grab my trusty sandals. But this was not the scene for them. The trail still had icy patches from the previous season, with the trees protecting it from the Sun's warmth.

I cursed and cursed, dreading the idea that we would instead drive the entire way up. I let out a sigh and caved into my defeat. "It's okay. We'll come back again and do the hike, but for now, we'll just drive." Despite my disappointment, my partner attempted to make the most out of a bad situation. We drove to the top, and it didn't make the sight any less beautiful. From the observation deck, you're able to see 360-degree mountain views of western North Carolina and beyond. I couldn't believe how far I could see. Nothing ever made me feel as small as standing above those hills.

I have ventured to Roan Mountain, part of the Roan Highlands on the border of western North Carolina and Tennessee, a handful of times.

Among the flora is the Catawba rhododendron. It thrives in this environment, creating the world's largest natural rhododendron garden. As if the views weren't enough reason to visit, the seasonal flower party was a popular attraction. I found myself roaming around Round Bald during the summer and autumn to catch the crimson-colored rhododendrons after thriving in their purple dresses.

As we hike down these high summits, the slopes inhabit some of the world's oldest growth. A playground for naturalists and animists alike, the woods offer one of the most diverse ecosystems and spirits. The Blue Ridge Mountains have a similar climate to that of a rainforest that quenches the thirst of abundant native trees and flora. As you hike through most paths, you'll be welcomed by towering trees like the American chestnut, Fraser fir, yellow birch, mountain ash, and eastern hemlock, as well as various pines and oaks. Living closer to the ground, you'll find flowering shrubs and smaller trees like the North Carolina state flower, dogwood, as well as mountain laurel, sourwood, and sassafras.

The mountaineer is familiar with the mountain laurel. Their photogenic flowers attract both locals and visitors as they paint the scene with their delicate blossoms in blushing ballet-pink. They serve as a natural shelter and create the perfect hideaway, growing as tall as trees and having long twig branches. Despite their beauty, they have another side that's quite wicked, with their toxic seeds and leaves. Their widespread branches and dense thickets granted them a reputation known as "laurel hell." If you accidentally tripped and fell into them, you'd spend forever fighting your way back.

Additionally, mountain ash is a personal favorite. Stemming from the same vein as the rose family, its lore runs deep through time and soil. Its European cousin was most known to be a tree of protection and healing, while also being associated with figures such as the devil and witches. With their blood-red berries shining bright against the dead shrubbery, I was immediately attracted to this spirit prior to diving into its stories. Though used mainly to protect cattle and the home, the wood is also used to protect against witchery. A charm with roots from the British Isles consists of two twigs tied together in the form of a cross bound by red thread. During my last home visit, we had hiked up the knob where my partner and I stated our vows, just as the mountain ash berries were ripest. I collected some in a mason jar, for a memento of home and to use for future protection workings.

We now meet where rivers snake their way through these foothills. I am most familiar with the French Broad River, which flows from Transylvania County of North Carolina to Knox County of Tennessee. It's fed by other rivers, such as the Swannanoa River in Buncombe County and Nolichucky River in Cocke County, before meeting the Tennessee River that flows into the Ohio River. To join, we have the Cumberland River in Harlon County of Kentucky, which is a major source for the Tennessee River. This river is about 680 miles long and extends westward of the mountain range. It weaves through the mountains of Kentucky and provides a picturesque scene of the Cumberland Falls. It continues north of Tennessee before weaving back into the Land Between the Lakes National Recreational Area, then merges with the Ohio River. I provide this picture of various rivers because they provided transportation and resources, as well as a sacred place for healing and cleansing rituals. They are also home to folktales of cryptids.

A particularly intriguing story is of the siren of the French Broad River. Having grown up close to this river, there were plenty of stories I overheard of its deep waters. Some that have you questioning whether to take a swim or not. Charles M. Skinner's 1896 collection of American folktales, *Myths and Legends of Our Own Land*, includes the Cherokee tale of the French Broad's siren:

> Among the rocks east of Asheville, North Carolina, lives the Lorelei of the French Broad River. This stream—the Tselica of the Indians—contains in its upper reaches many pools where the rapid water whirls and deepens, and where the traveller likes to pause in the heats of afternoon and drink and bathe. Here, from the time when the Cherokees occupied the country, has lived the siren, and if one who is weary and downcast sits beside the stream or utters a wish to rest in it, he becomes conscious of a soft and exquisite music blending with the plash of the wave.
>
> Looking down in surprise he sees—at first faintly, then with distinctness—the form of a beautiful woman, with hair streaming like moss and dark eyes looking into his, luring him with a power he cannot resist. His breath grows short, his gaze is fixed, mechanically he rises, steps to the brink, and lurches forward into the river. The arms that catch him are slimy and cold as serpents; the face that stares into his is a grinning skull. A loud, chattering laugh rings through the wilderness, and all is still again.

Tales of the rivers don't stop there. Not only were they filled with mythical beings such as sirens, but also the devil himself. One of great popularity resides in the Nolichucky River with the Devil's Looking Glass towering just above it in Unicoi County. For generations, locals have shared the Cherokee stories of a woman jumping from the cliff into the waters below in sorrow of her lost lover. Locals continue to record longing cries and wailings of what sounds like a woman crying when camping nearby. The name of the cliff, Devil's Looking Glass, comes from the moonlight's shadows from the water below. The reflection appears to be a window into another realm, or the "seven faces of demons." Then, there are tales where the devil himself crossed the river, leaving behind hooved footprints.

When you sit back and look at these views from the front porch, there's so much that the natural landscape has to offer for those seeking to foster a relationship with it. Filled with tales as old as time and home to diverse species and spirits, this landscape is an antique clock reminding us of those before etched in each wooded pathway. There are views that can't quite be properly captured by written words. They're meant to be experienced. They're welcoming, yet mysterious and looming with a sense of depth that defies easy explanation. Trees offer privacy to retreat, and the rivers invite us to take a breath. What appears to be a peaceful reserve is much deeper and more multifaceted than the outsider's eye.

By the People

The ancestry of southern Appalachia consists of diverse cultures coming together, each weaving into the land and its people. The region's major influences come from Indigenous Peoples, European immigrants, and enslaved African descendants, delivering a rich amalgamation of traditions, healing practices, and folkways. We won't go back to the beginning, as that would take quite a bit of time. But I will do my best to offer an understanding of the *folk* behind southern Appalachia's ways and magic.

Long before European immigrants arrived in the mountains, the region was the ancestral and current home to Indigenous Peoples. The tribes within the southern Appalachian region include the Cherokee, Shawnee, Catawba, and many more. These nations already had established working towns and societal systems before colonization. They thrived off the land, cultivating trading relationships with fellow tribes, and created successful agricultural practices. Their spirituality is rooted in their relationship with the land—a connection that colonialism has attempted to disrupt. The Indigenous folktales of Appalachia are deeply engrained in this landscape. They are passed down not only to preserve history, but also to highlight the various land spirits that reside here. Much of the region's folklore originates from their stories, especially when connecting with natural landmarks such as rivers, mountains, lakes, forests, and beyond. The Indigenous Peoples' herbal knowledge built the foundation of herbal medicine in the region's folk healing practices. They taught European immigrants and enslaved African people how to work with native plants in their wellness care. Without this knowledge-able exchange, many would have been unable to develop agricultural or natural health-care needs in the New World.

The British Isles had their historic annexation occurring at the same time as the settlement of the New World, beginning in the early 17th century with the Plantation of Ulster. Most of these settlers came to Northern Ireland from the Lowland Scottish and English borders. The Borderers, as they were called, were known to not have loyalty to one side over the other, as many had relatives on both sides. Instead, their blood ran off the constant pressure between the two lands, often resulting in raids without political direction. Their fierceness and combative nature positioned them as a continuous threat against the British Crown. This tension led to the power move of displacing them to Northern Ireland.

Many of these Borderers adapted to fit into Northern Ireland, yet there were still tensions with the new neighbors. In some cases, during outbreaks of political powers and wars, the Ulster Scots fought alongside their Irish neighbors to protect land and religious rights. The second wave of Scottish settlers came to Northern Ireland after fleeing the seven-year famine. The

Scottish sought refuge, resources, and safety after continuous failed crops and rising food prices. Between rising religious tensions and desire for new opportunities, a mass exodus followed, and the Ulster Scots, or Scots-Irish, became one of the largest European groups to migrate to the New World in the early 18th century. They brought their families, strong faith, ballads, and traditions that became another thread in the mountain region's intricate quilt.

The German immigrants share a similar story and were another large European diaspora that made the migration beginning in the 17th century. They left their homeland in search of refuge from warfare, economic hardships, and religious pressures. The majority of German families immigrated to northern Appalachia and established close-knit German-speaking communities around major cities like Pittsburgh, where they became known as the Pennsylvania Dutch. Their vibrant communities focused on preserving their ancestral traditions, which were influential in Appalachian culture. Eventually, opportunities became competitive and scarce in the north, leading German-American families to migrate further south into Virginia and the Carolinas, establishing themselves in these southern hills. Their traditions like the Pennsylvania Dutch healing practice of Braucherei took root. Their practices such as planting by the zodiac signs, healing remedies, and divination methods were adopted into the region's magical landscape.

The African peoples' experience in these mountains is a story that involves enslavement, migration, and resilience. The descendants of enslaved Africans play a significant role in shaping the southern Appalachian culture and folk magic, a fact that deserves closer examination. The people who had been ripped from their homelands of west and central Africa were forced across the Atlantic under inhumane conditions. The misconception that these hills were composed solely of "poor white working-class families" erases the historical contributions of Black and African American peoples. These mountains were not immune to the rest of the colonial country's flaws. Historical records reveal in western North Carolina that forced labor of enslaved African people compromised about two-fifths of the working population outside agriculture.

After the Civil War, freed African Americans relocated from the Deep South to seek working opportunities in Appalachia's coal mining industry. They brought along their survived spiritual and religious practices, as well as herbal medicine. Their spiritual practices, rooted in African traditional religions, intertwined with the dominant faith of their oppressors to carefully disguise within the Christian framework for preservation. Many African descendants in the southern region adopted Catholicism or Protestantism, often out of necessity or coercion. However, they preserved elements of their ancestral spirituality, leading to the birth of folk practices such as Hoodoo. Their traditions significantly influence the cultural blend of Appalachian folk magic. To ignore or disregard the influence of the African diaspora in this region is to disregard a vital piece of southern Appalachian culture.

As you can see, the intersection of these three significant cultures—Indigenous Peoples, African, and European—set the stage for a unique culture that authentically speaks for itself: the dishes served, ballads sung, folktales told, healing remedies used, prayers spoken, and spiritual traditions. As the New World shifted, so did the way people interacted with one another. Cultural exchanges occurred as a natural result of intermingling between the people. The folk traditions adopted a diasporic identity shaped by their new region and neighbors. It is no longer just Indigenous, African, or European after encountering one another; these traditions transmuted and adapted over time into the culture that now exists in the people of Appalachia.

By the Government

The government's definition of southern Appalachia is shaped by its history. From the Civil War and the subsequent industrial boom to the struggles of the Great Depression, the region's history has significantly influenced both its government and its people. These historical chapters highlight Appalachia's resilience, despairs, and shared experiences, reflecting the exchanged traditions contributing to these mountains' unique magic.

The Civil War was one of the most severe conflicts that impacted the region socially and economically. Due to polarizing political and societal stances, recorded cases of individuals fighting on both sides exist. Families and neighbors were divided, with not one person being strictly loyal to the other due to differentiating views. The conflict—this Brothers' War— divided families and communities, pitting relatives and neighbors against one another. In John Alexander Williams's work, *Appalachia: A History*, he describes such circumstances:

> In East Tennessee and southwest Virginia, there were men who returned home either as Confederate deserters or as veterans whose enlistments had expired, and who then fled over the mountains into Kentucky and the federal army rather than surrender to the Confederate draft. Farther south—in western North Carolina and north Georgia—rebel deserters and Union volunteers enlisted in Tennessee units after the Federals took control there in late 1863. Differences in timing as well as opinion also explain something of the "brothers' war" of Civil War sentimentalists: An older brother might march off with his buddies as the local militia was mustered into Confederate service, while a younger one would face different circumstances and options when he came of age a year or two

later. Such innocent logic could lead to decades, even generations, of bitterness within and between families after war.

While siblings and neighbors clashed over polarizing perspectives, the rugged landscape became the perfect battleground. The repetitive hills allowed soldiers to execute strategic surprise attacks on their opponents. Deforestation permanently scarred the region to create these battlegrounds. The hills still bear the marks of countless confrontations, including the tactical efforts to block railroad bridges in the Cumberland Mountains and disrupt supply chains. Amidst an already fragile economy, the Civil War exacerbated the turmoil as men enlisted in the war left their businesses, families, and homes behind.

As a result, industries shifted to meet the war's increased demand for natural resources, particularly coal. The coal mining industry became one of the most significant drivers of industrialization in the region following the Civil War. Appalachia, rich in "black gold," attracted large outsider extraction companies to the area, seeking to exploit the land and the people for monetary gain. Coal was essential for powering steam engines, producing iron and steel for tools, and fueling factories. The extraction industry thrived, producing some of the most extensive mining operations and camps in the southern Appalachian region.

After the Civil War, families were recovering from either losing loved ones or the loss of their farms, businesses, or homes. The ripple effects of the war impacted people's decisions on how to go about life in this new era. With the economic shifts, people began accepting large corporation job opportunities in the rapidly growing industry. It was pitched as a great opportunity for families and to those interested in pursuing a life in America. Corporations began recruiting local Appalachians and immigrants from Italy, Germany, Poland, Eastern European nations, and elsewhere to meet high production demands. The miners and their families would reside in company-owned housing within the company-owned coal camps. The family's size didn't matter when it came to provided housing; all houses had the same structure. Large corporations were cautious of the potential of organized unions among miners, so they segregated, housing by ethnicity. But that didn't affect the brotherhood between miners and their families within the coal camps. Women showed remarkable unity and support for each other in challenging conditions. They leaned on one another for domestic support, creating communal gatherings such as "wash days," where they'd help each other in the labor-intensive task of washing the clothes of their coal mining partners while socializing simultaneously. They nurtured gardens together along the backwoods of campsites due to land limitations for growing their own food supply. Differences subsided, and alliances formed between families that endured similar struggles.

The idea of building financial stability drove many families' decision to work for these corporations. Jobs were hard to come by, especially ones that offered housing, and the coal industry was booming with attractive opportunities. However, these large coal companies weren't handing out dollar bills for the workers' hard labor. Instead, companies paid in company-owned money called *scrip*. This company money could only be used to purchase goods at verified stores within the coal camps. The restrictions on receiving financial compensation that could be used outside the local areas only further isolated coal miners and their families. This prevented working class families from building wealth and moving up in other industries. They were highly dependent on the coal companies to provide a sense of security despite harsh working conditions that had lasting health effects.

The coal mining industry sucked the life out of the mountains and the people, bearing some of the deepest and darkest folklore. The horrifying working conditions were fuel to the fire as many miners succumbed to fatal illnesses, such as black lung. Without any labor laws in place, kids as young as seven worked long hours alongside their working parents. The young miners were positioned as trappers and breakers, as their petite size allowed them to fit into crevices. These job roles consisted of long hours in cramped, dark, and damp environments that were the source of rising illnesses in these young miners. The machinery operated by miners was also hazardous if not handled correctly. The results could be catastrophic accidental explosions that cost the lives of those working deep in the mountain's belly.

Tensions between miners and large corporations steadily escalated due to the exploitation of laborers. Inspired by the formation of unions in other states, miners began organizing strikes at local camps against their employers. This unrest soon led to the Mine Wars in the early 20th century. These regional battles between miners and employers eventually prompted intervention from local governments. Coal miners from diverse backgrounds unified their efforts to negotiate better working conditions and fair compensation. This wave of activism led to the formation of the United Mine Workers of America (UMWA), a union created to support miners in negotiating with large corporations on issues such as pay, working conditions, hours, and job security. The UMWA played a crucial role in organizing strikes to apply pressure on corporations. Some strikes, such as the infamous Battle of Blair Mountain in Logan County, West Virginia, turned violent. This dramatic confrontation drew national attention and led to federal intervention. The Battle of Blair Mountain became one of American history's most significant and influential labor uprisings, highlighting the fight for workers' rights and the continued suppression of labor disruption.

Following the Mine Wars, new challenges loomed for the southern mountaineer. The Great Depression of the 1930s struck hard, deepening the existing social class divides of the working class and causing widespread hardship across the country. In an isolated region, the economic downturn had limited government assistance, intensifying the local distress. The decline of the prominent coal mining industry coincided with the upswing of other natural resources and newly implemented climate control laws. Appalachians who depended on job security were now left astray. The failure of extraction companies led to major layoffs and abandoned towns, leaving miners and their families in despair. The conditions of the agricultural industry were equally dire; plummeting product prices led to widespread foreclosures and loss of land. What had been a hopeful chapter became an era of great hardship. People clung to their faith and relied on their neighbors, finding solace in the small blessings of having a roof over their heads and bread on the table.

As a result of these dire times, images of Appalachian towns were exploited in the national spotlight. The mass media showcased long breadlines and distressed housing conditions. It brought to the attention of the rest of the country a region that was hurting and forgotten. As a response, the War on Poverty was issued as an effort to provide federal government assistance and initiate programs to address the region's economic inequalities.

Based on similar economic hardships, the government created specific boundaries that would be supported by the Appalachian Regional Commission, or ARC, spanning thirteen states and over four hundred counties. The map defined by ARC covers southern counties of New York, western Pennsylvania, and southeastern Ohio, all of West Virginia, western Virginia and North Carolina, eastern Tennessee, and northern counties of South Carolina, Georgia, Alabama, and even Mississippi. This federal partnership was created to provide aid in recovering counties across Appalachia. The responsive initiative focuses on investing in economic development, infrastructure, education development, health care, and more.

Though the government had its own agenda of intervening and improving the lives of Appalachians, the people did not forget. This history is embedded in everything we do and our outlook on life. It has left a lasting scar—one that requires continued nurturing attention. That is not to say there haven't been any improvements. Since the start of ARC, Appalachia's poverty rate has been halved over the past five and a half decades. To keep people up to date on the region's statistics as a result of ARC's ongoing work, they share updated data reports every fiscal year that are worth reviewing.

There are still concerning issues, however—specifically the ongoing battle with pharmaceutical companies and opioid-related mortality rates. Recent data show that these specific health issues are higher in Appalachia than elsewhere in the country. The region continues to have fewer health-care resources, making access to health care a longstanding challenge in rural counties. This shortage has created opportunities for local medicine healers to continue their work and serve their communities. While there has been progress compared to previous generations, there is still a long road ahead.

As a granddaughter of Kentucky farmers and coal miners, I try to see things through their eyes. It helps gain perspective by placing myself in their shoes and considering their struggles and grievances, and how these ancestral experiences may present themselves through certain behaviors in my life today. Observing these historical moments that greatly impacted the past and the present has allowed me to understand the folkways and magic that emerged. It has been instrumental in healing generational wounds that continue to show up in a pattern, including a scarcity mindset from the traumas experienced by previous family members.

Growing up in western North Carolina, I witnessed my hometown beginning to be stripped of its resources. Affordable housing and fair-paying jobs became increasingly scarce. This mirrored the experience of my past ancestors. The changes my hometown underwent led to the difficult decision to relocate. Sometimes, I think that the mountains had planned that scenario for me as a personal lesson. In a conversation with a beloved friend about my grief moving away from home, she reassured me in making this decision, commenting matter-of-factly, "If that ain't Appalachian, I don't know what is."

2

ON FRONT PORCHES AND IN GARDEN BEDS: FOLKWAYS OF THE SOUTHERN MOUNTAINEER

Reflecting on family memories, I find only a few bright and lively moments remain clear, yet they resemble an Appalachian upbringing. Many of these memories are set in my grandparents' South Carolina log cabin, around kitchen tables, in front of fireplaces, and on front porches overlooking lawns with distant forests. They were not elaborate settings, by any means, but places that held significant personal meaning.

When we moved back to North Carolina, my mother opened a quilting store in Flat Rock. The building was a weathered stone-colored cabin with two levels and all hardwood flooring. A short pathway led to the front porch with rocking chairs and the main entrance. Hot pink azaleas and other blossoms welcomed customers in the front garden, with tall sunflowers guarding just around the corner. There was an open field in the back filled with abundant wildflowers and tall grass, and a narrow man-made trail that led to who knows where.

My mother named it The Quilting Corner.

I was no stranger to the shop. I'd see the large storefront sign from the highway, with the Sister's Choice quilting block in all four corners. My father had built the store's wooden cutting table and ordered custom shelving to fit the wide selection of fabrics displayed in nearly every room. The bolts of fabric were neatly organized in a system that only my mother and her friends understood. For me, it was a sensory playground to touch everything and examine the many printed patterns. Hung high from the ceiling for all to see were finished quilts to demonstrate the richness of this craft. So many different patterns, colors, and fabrics telling a story through the art of thread and needle. A physical, and rather comfortable if washed well, testimony to the craft and the people.

My mother hosted quilt shows, guilds, and classes, a few of which I attended. My job was simple: stamp everyone's Shop-Hop booklet, fetch missing supplies, place a bolt of fabric back in the right place. As I'd sit in the corner, the buzzing of sewing machines and chatter would fill the room. The shop was more than just a place to buy fabric, thread, buttons, or patterns. It had become a community where all generations of quilters gathered, consulted, and collaborated. Amidst the hums, I'd hear tidbits of family stories, of old friends catching up, and new friendships blossoming. It was the stitch that tied many people together.

While my mother chose needle and thread for her interest, my father was a man who took on the hobby of canning. He had purchased countless Ball mason jars and lids along with the best high-pressure cooker on the market. One year, he had gotten a hold of some Kentucky Wonder green beans, some of the "absolute best," he'd say. There we sat with bushels of green beans ready to be stripped. The stripping of the green beans took ages, and young me would grow tirelessly bored by the constant motion. We'd sit there for hours in the living room during a warm afternoon, just tending to the green beans, one at a time. "It'll be worth it," my father remarked, and he was right. Our labor had paid off because they were the finest canned green beans I've ever had to this day. We canned enough together to last us through the winter months until my father could get his hands on those green beans again. I remember we'd preserve them for as long as possible, keeping the last cans for special occasions only.

If one quality defines southern mountaineers, it's their profound appreciation for simplicity. For a length of time, simplicity was the way. They valued practicality, putting to good use resources that were easily available, and learned new, sustainable ways to make life a little easier. I've seen this demonstrated in my own family line. We don't like for things to go to waste—we use up what we've already got—and sometimes our independence can come off as a little stubborn. "You're just so independent," I'd hear growing up. But that's just how I learned to get things done.

This mindset, cultivated from an earlier time, shapes how generations of Appalachian folk approach everything from family traditions to daily routines to their craftsmanship. In this section, we'll explore how the backbone of southern mountain life—its beginning homesteads, food, ballads, arts, and faith—has influenced the folk magic unique to this region. Since we've briefly covered the region's history, which heavily impacted the lives of common folk, we now explore the rich culture born in this patchwork-quilted landscape. We acknowledge the foundations that influenced those before us and create a bridge for those seeking to reconnect with their roots. We offer a reintroduction to the culture that shapes Appalachian identity. This is a glimpse into some of the folkways as a starting point. There are countless ways to embrace Appalachian culture. My hope is that this sparks an old memory or inspires you to dip your toes into something new.

THE HOMESTEAD

When we think of the early mountaineers, it's easy to picture a rustic log cabin perched on a hilltop among the misty mountains. It's one that you may have seen before. The scene evokes a sense of nostalgia for a life grounded in nature. It feels both timeless and raw. A legacy carved from those embarking on the unfamiliar path. The image of a cabin overlooking a mountain view has become somewhat of a trademark of the region's past. Some solid foundations have sustained the weathered passing of time. Others have become generational homes, passed down to children and grandchildren who make modern improvements over time. Sometimes, you'll come across cabins that were left behind. These are the ones that have quite the collection of stories to tell if you give them the time of day to talk. They stand as a testimony to the families that built them from the ground up, much like their new lives. These homesteads were more than a place that provided shelter from an unpredictable outside world. They were the framework for a future, built by the hope that guided them from across land and sea with their bare hands.

The German immigrants taught their neighbors their distinct building techniques of dovetail notching to ensure log homes could withstand the harsh mountain climate. They were constructed by cutting down oak or chestnut trees from the wooded grounds. These log homes were strategically positioned in close proximity to water sources and transportation routes. It was also helpful to build on higher elevations to overlook the property, just in case of any wandering strangers. Inside the log home was a simple layout. The hearth had an open firepit for cooking, a small space for family gatherings, and a separate area strictly used for sleeping. Home constructions weren't as lavish as we see them nowadays. It wasn't until housing construction laws were passed in the twentieth century that layouts could be more complex, with expanded rooms and modernized floor plans that we see today.

Due to the colonial cabin's size limitations, separate outbuildings served specific needs. Some families designated their outbuilding for milk production and storage, while others utilized it as a washhouse, springhouse, or smokehouse. Since the family's primary meat source was the pig, they needed a designated area to butcher and adequately preserve the meat.

A smokehouse was precisely that. Smokehouses are famously used today for Southern cooking—an example of how some traditions never truly die, but instead grow and become an ode to older ways.

Besides the cabin quarters, there was usually a barn to shelter the homestead's animals as a source of food and earnings. Cows were often kept for milk and to help with labor but rarely as a primary food source. In Kephart's *Our Southern Highlanders*, he writes that the mountaineer who lived high in the hills didn't find much value in keeping cows for personal sake but instead in exporting them or selling the meat for whatever they could to their neighbors. There wasn't much for the cow to graze on in the elevated cliffs. They thrived down in the valleys where the vegetation was more nourishing. Other animals, such as horses and mules, assisted the farmers' work by pulling wagons to transport wood and crops. Chickens were also present for food and monetary purposes. However, the most valuable animal a family could own was the pig. They required minimal upkeep and often roamed freely on the hill and grazed to their heart's content. Pigs were the primary food source for southern mountaineers, and every part of the animal was put to good use for home-cooked meals and baking.

Overlooking the mountaineer's homestead, their true labor of love lies in the garden's soil. It served as their main source of food as well as income. Selecting a suitable spot for the garden was no small undertaking. The mountaineer understood that the soil needed to be rich and accessible to the Sun's warmth for the perfect balanced foundation. By the 20th century, the garden featured a diverse list of native crops and old world imported goods. Corn, for example, is a native crop that was grown successfully by the Cherokee, who taught the newcomers. Corn was a nutritious source for signature dishes, but new seed varieties introduced through trade and migration expanded the menu. In the summer, the garden would flourish with red ripe tomatoes, crisp green beans, crunchy carrots, and vines of peas. Onions, Irish potatoes, and sweet potatoes awaited underground. Other root crops were introduced that could bear the higher altitudes and unpredictable weather patterns, such as cabbage, turnips, lettuces, and collards. The mountaineer's garden was their pride and joy, as it provided more than nourishment for their family. Abundance was shared with the neighbors. They'd exchange one good for another, whether it was a basket of tomatoes for homemade jam, or collard greens for a carton of eggs. Abundance wasn't singular, but something to be shared.

There's been a recent movement to return to self-sustainable practices where folks take their gardens more seriously. Now more than ever, I have felt called to return to such sustainable approaches. As I write this, I may not have much yard, but that doesn't prevent me from seeking alternatives. Potatoes can be grown in small container bins, and herbs can be stored along the windowsill. This helps with grocery costs and allows for more intimate relationship-building with common herbs and plants found in folk magic.

Beyond the practicalities of gardening, the soil holds profound spiritual significance for Appalachian practitioners. The practices of gardening and magic can intertwine in various ways. Gardeners take special note of the seasonal shifts in the same way practitioners plan rituals according to nature's cycles. They both pay close attention to the natural world to communicate when seeds are meant to be planted, while others are harvested and then prepped for a long slumber in the darker months. The relationship between crop and gardener is a mirror of plant and practitioner. Farmwork and gardening can be a ritual in itself. Planting the seeds represents planting new beginnings. A consented relationship with a plant spirit in the garden may guide the practitioner's work. In exchange for attentive care, the plant spirit may offer lessons in patience, perseverance, and bearing fruits after a season of hard labor—all worthy lessons that can be applied in other areas of the practitioner's life. A spiritually devoted garden can be used for preparing healing tinctures, homecooked intentional meals, protective charms, and food offerings for other spirits.

DOWN THE RABBIT HOLE
The Old Farmer's Almanac

Perhaps you've dabbled a bit in gardening yourself, as many folk practitioners find themselves called to do, whether for self-sustaining purposes, medicinal healing remedies, charm making, spirit contracts, or otherwise. Regardless of how you find yourself on the green path, the almanac is the gardener's bible. William Pierce from England published the first edition of the almanac in the New World called *An Almanack Calculated for New England*. Its contents included a series of informative local news stories about the region, astronomical forecasts, weather patterns, and planting guides. The almanac industry had officially begun due to its popularity with locals, and it caught on quickly with useful information for daily life.

As the industry grew, more almanacs were printed. Benjamin Franklin published a series called *Poor Richard's Almanack* under his pen name, Richard Saunders, which contained not only weather information but also humorous writings and proverbs. The intent of the publication then expanded into offering more than just the astronomical and weather forecast for farmers. It also provided community information about local events and entertainment, as well as jokes and comics. Home remedy articles in

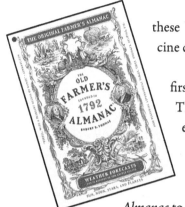

these books helped local folk strengthen their medicine cabinets with accessible and simple recipes.

The almanac we are most familiar with today was first published in the 19th century by Robert Bailey Thomas and was called *The Farmer's Almanac*. This edition has become the most popular despite the numerous editions published by other authors. It is the longest-surviving almanac and was granted the official title of *The Old Farmer's Almanac* to establish its lasting legacy.

A traditional way of farming adopted into the folk practices of German immigrants was planting by the zodiac signs and lunar phases. A graphic is included in *The Old Farmer's Almanac* for farmers and gardeners to refer to for planning. As folk practitioners, we often utilize this same concept to connect deeper with the celestial energy of the stars in the sky and our friend the Moon. Referencing the zodiac sign of the Moon can help determine the best astrological timing for magical workings and rituals.

Planting by the zodiac signs involves timing gardening activities to align with the astrological characteristics of each sign, optimizing potential plant growth and soil health by leveraging the traits associated with each zodiac sign, such as stability, fertility, and nourishment. The most favored zodiac signs for gardening are Cancer, Taurus, Scorpio, Pisces, and Capricorn. A commonality among all five signs is that they are ruled either by the element of water or by the element of earth. Taurus, for example, is an earth element zodiac sign that is associated with the planet Venus. It also corresponds to the neck of the human body. Taurus provides the ideal energy for sturdy root vegetables and fertile soil because the sign is associated with fertility, stability, and abundance. As for Cancer, it is a water element zodiac sign that is ruled by the Moon and corresponds to the chest and stomach.

This energy is incredibly nourishing, as Cancer is most known for having a motherly nature. Being ruled by water, produce like watermelons and cantaloupes favor being planted under this zodiac sign. Other gardening tasks are associated with corresponding zodiac signs within the calendar year. For example, Aries is a fire element zodiac sign that is the first in the astrological calendar. When the Sun is positioned in this season, it is an ideal time to begin cultivating the soil in preparation for planting seeds and removing any weeds.

Planting by the Moon phase is also a practice that many still adhere to today. It is suggested for successful growth of vegetables that bear crops above the surface to plant during the cycle from the New Moon until the Full Moon, also known as the Waxing Moon period. This Moon cycle visually represents growth as the Moon grows in its fullness and brightness. The opposite is recommended for vegetables that bear crops below the ground; ideal planting should be after the Full Moon and before the upcoming New Moon during the waning period.

Whether you believe in fate being in the hands of the stars or not, early Appalachian folks attempted anything that would lend a helping hand for a bountiful harvest. If you've not taken this approach before, I recommend getting your hands dirty and putting it to the test. Keep in mind that your exact location and climate will vary depending on the zone in which you're gardening. Pick up a current *Old Farmer's Almanac* for more information about your location and planting timeline recommendations.

FROM FARM TO TABLE

In an Appalachian home, gatherings in the kitchen are an orchestrated symphony. Someone would be tending the biscuit dough while another prepared the meat in the smokehouse. Someone would be on potato peeling duty while someone else would prep the cast-iron pot for supper's stew.

The rhythmic chopping of vegetables, the steady hum of quick orders and gentle banter, and the occasional clatter of stoneware created a comforting clamor of a busy home. The kitchen became a hub of warmth and togetherness, where each task was a note in the ballad of preparing a hearty meal. This is all too familiar to me. The kitchen was not only designated for home cooking, but also back pats and belly laughs.

The heart of an Appalachian kitchen is forged in cast iron—strong, durable, loyal, and always up to the task. Cast iron is symbolic of both culinary tradition and familial legacy. With its iron strength, it withstands the hottest of temperatures and it only gets better with age. Generations have passed their cast iron down, each layer of seasoning a chapter in the family story. I acquired my first cast iron from my brother when he was cleaning out his houseware items. It was a small, square cast-iron skillet that needed some love and care. It served me well before I invested in a larger skillet that rests on the stovetop with leftover bacon grease.

Now, I assume that if you're reading this book, you are familiar with Southern food or at least know of its reputation. There isn't anything like it. Since relocating to the Pacific Northwest, it is by far the one thing I miss the most. Not because I am skilled at cooking but because my friends and neighbors who invited me over blessed my taste buds like no other place has. There truly is comfort in every bite. As I write this, my mouth craves some of my favorite food spots back home. Fluffy biscuits with juicy peach rosemary jam. Fried hot chicken with house-made ranch and baked mac 'n cheese with green bean casserole. Sweet barbecue ribs with corn pudding. Smooth, sweet banana pudding with vanilla wafers and whipped cream on top. Whenever I miss my comfort dishes, I'll retreat to the kitchen in hopes of successfully recreating them.

We can graciously thank the Cherokee for inspiring a Southern staple, cornbread. Sure, you may think that's cliché, but I find myself baking it for instant fulfillment. It brings great comfort and has become one of my ancestor's preferred food offerings. The Cherokee used the thriving corn crop and developed ways to cultivate, process, and cook it into traditional dishes. The Cherokee's cooking methods inspired many of our staple side dishes such as fritters, griddle cakes, and, yes, even cornbread. Corn continues to be an essential part of a Southern plate. African descendants and the Indigenous Peoples came into early contact with one another and developed a common bond over the agricultural realm. The result was an exchange of traditional dishes presented on most household dinner plates. Black chefs and their innovative recipes were foundational to many early Southern cookbooks, appearing in both white and Black households. They skillfully incorporated native crops, blending African culinary customs with herbs and spices, profoundly shaping the modern Southern food scene.

Though cornbread is perhaps one's favorite (or maybe I'm just projecting my own feelings here), fluffy biscuits are also very popular. Depending on who's Mamaw you ask, the recipe will vary from family to family. This is one of those instances when I sincerely wish I had a generational recipe book. Perhaps there is one hidden under dust that has yet to be uncovered that I could get my hands on.

During the Civil War, cathead biscuits became a tradition as key ingredients became more accessible. These biscuits are made with flour, lard, buttermilk, salt, baking soda, and baking powder. The ingredients are combined to make the batter and then crafted by hand into a round form the same size as a cat's head; hence, the name. The biscuits are enjoyed throughout the day and served with sweet honey jam or sawmill sausage gravy. They provided the nutrients workers would need to sustain them for forty-plus-hour workweeks in the mines, farms, or factories. Biscuit recipes have transformed over time, with each family adding their own unique flavors and specialties.

Dumplings are another traditional dish that reflects the cultural intersection of the South. Made from a simple mixture of flour, salt, and water, they stretched meals and enriched dinner stews. Though dumpling dishes of all kinds were present before the New World, the dish was reintroduced with new flavors that vary with who's behind the stovetop. I've enjoyed savory chicken and dumplings during the winter season as a soul-warming meal the same way I've enjoyed them sweet with baked apples and cinnamon as a little afternoon treat.

In my research of familial stories, my father shared with me old footage of his grandmother, Mamaw Nora, and his grandfather, Papaw Alexander. The video had been digitized to share it around. You can barely make out the black-and-white picture of them standing in the kitchen, with the focus being on Mamaw Nora. But her voice is as clear as day. Sometimes, I wonder if I'd had the pleasure of having her around during childhood if I'd have picked up the songbird melody of her words. Like myself, she was a petite woman, just under five feet tall. The woman beside her, a family member I'm unfamiliar with, asked her what was for dinner. She spelled it all out: "We're havin' chicken 'n dumplings . . . beans and potatoes . . . cornbread . . . green beans . . . onion and carrots. . . ." Mamaw Nora glances over at the camera with a chuckle, knowing full well the length of her menu. Family rumors say that everyone's favorite was Mamaw Nora's fried apple pies and green beans.

The southern Appalachian culinary landscape is diverse and deeply comforting, serving not just as a reflection of our ancestors' hard-earned bounty but as a cherished means of welcoming neighbors and family into their homes. A warm meal, made with love, resulted in a full belly as you relaxed on the sofa before the fireplace for evening banter. By savoring these traditional dishes, we're tasting both the past and present. These recipes are a testament to the various homelands that were left behind. The region's culinary scene continues to grow, blending the old practices with fresh influ-ences. In the simplicity of a recipe, we catch glimpses of our ancestors' daily lives. The contents of their cupboards, the crops from their homesteads, and the fuel that helped sustain them through harsh times. It's become the country's best-known region for good, comfort food dishes. Incorporating ancestral traditional dishes into our current plates directly connects us to their spirits. It feeds them as much as it feeds us. Southern food is a story of perseverance and good flavor to be shared with good company.

FROM MAMAW'S BOOK OF SPELLS:
Apple Jam and Biscuits for Connection

This simple recipe is meant to be shared with beloved folks and spirits of yours. The intended focus is to use ingredients that correspond to *connec-tion*, *love*, and *companionship*. I was inspired by my Mamaw Nora and her popular flavored apple pies to perfect a personal apple jam recipe that I'd consider passing down. So far, that would include you. Make this recipe as a food offering, to be shared at the kitchen table, or as a gift to someone special.

To make the kitchen suitable for a magical working, I like to physically clean and spiritually cleanse beforehand. I will invite my ancestor spirits into the space when cooking something inspired by my home region. This looks like lighting a dedicated candle to guide their spirit into the shared space and reciting a prayer. One I like to say goes like this: "Ancestors of blood and bone, of the wise and well, those who guide and protect me along this path—I invite you to join me." If you have an ancestor in mind who was quite clever in

the world of cooking, invite them by saying their name. Throughout the cooking process, remain open to any intuitive guidance that may be felt. Sometimes, we'll feel a pull for a specific spice from the cabinet that we had not yet considered. There's a reason for that! I believe that is an ancestor's way of making a recommendation. Add it to your dish and see how it turns out.

If you can, source the apples from your local orchard around the autumnal season. I prefer Honeycrisp apples for this recipe, but feel free to use alternatives that suit your taste. Apples represent the spirit realm, ancestral connection, and life and death, and are often used in divination practices. For example, a branch from an apple tree can be used as a divination rod for water witching. Apple trees were also used by healers to help aid toothaches by plugging the sick person's fingernails and an eyelash into the tree trunk. You can also peel the apple's skin while reciting the alphabet as a divination practice. Should the strip break, the letter that you've come to is meant to be the first letter of your future love.

For the jam, you will need:

- 4–5 apples, depending on their size and how much of the jam you want to make

- ½ cup granulated sugar

- ½ cup brown sugar

- Ground cinnamon to taste (optional)

- Ground cloves to taste (optional)

- 1 tablespoon lemon juice

- Orange zest (optional)

To start, wash and peel the apples. Once all the apples are peeled, cut them into slices and place them in a saucepan over medium heat. Preserve the apple seeds in a jar for future workings and charms.

Add the granulated sugar and brown sugar to the pan. Stir clockwise, allowing the mixture to simmer and thicken. Then add the cinnamon and cloves to taste. (I don't normally determine the exact amount for spices because some folks are more sensitive than others. It's always "a little bit of this" and "a little bit of that." Or, if you don't like the spices at all, feel free to leave them out.) Next, add about a tablespoon of lemon juice. Lastly, add a bit of orange zest if you're feeling adventurous.

Once the mixture is thick, store it in a sanitized mason jar. Remember to date it and keep it in the refrigerator. It will keep up to six months, but once opened it is best consumed within three weeks while kept in the refrigerator.

For the cathead biscuits, you will need:

- 2 cups self-rising flour (any brand is fine)
- 2 tablespoons shortening
- 1 cup cold buttermilk, plus a little extra if needed

Preheat the oven to 475 degrees. To make the biscuits, combine the self-rising flour with about a tablespoon of shortening. Work the flour and shortening together until well combined with a fork or clean hands. Then slowly add 1 cup cold buttermilk while mixing. I find using my hands is best at this point. Combine well until it creates a sticky dough. If you need to add more buttermilk, that's fine. It should be a well-balanced dough, not too wet or too dry. Take a small handful and roll it into a ball the size of, well, a cat's head, and place on a lined sheet pan. Repeat with the remaining dough. You should have about five biscuits. Bake at 475 degrees for about 15 minutes or until the biscuits are golden brown.

I enjoy biscuits shortly after they're done in the oven when they're still warm. Slather on some of that apple jam with some butter and share it with others. If it is a food offering to spirits, I will leave them a small plate for the day, paying special close attention to avoid any ants during the summer months and keep out of reach of household pets.

FROM MAMAW'S BOOK OF SPELLS:
Wishbone Charm for Good Luck

Poultry is considered a granter of wishes. The use of a wishbone from a bird dates back to Italian practices when poultry bones were used for divination and good luck charms. But rather than pulling apart the wishbone of a sacrificed chicken or turkey, they would instead stroke the bone with a wish in mind.

This tradition was adapted as other regions took hold of this idea. In medieval Europe, breaking of the wishbone was performed for fun during the holiday season. In addition to being used for good luck charms, breaking the wishbone was a form of divination: The one who received the largest piece would be the one to marry next or be granted good fortune.

The wishbone continues to be used as a symbol of fortune, wish-granting, divination, and luck. I myself believe in the representation and even have a wishbone tattooed above my left elbow. Growing up, my father would keep the wishbone of the holiday turkey for us to pull apart, seeing who would get the bigger half as a fun holiday game rather than a wish granter. I've put the wishbone into practice to persuade luck to be on my side for certain matters, like career-related aspirations.

For this charm, you will need:

- A clean wishbone
- Blessed water
- A length of red thread, enough to wrap around the wishbone
- Blended mint and chamomile incense

I typically retrieve a wishbone from the local grocery store's rotisserie chicken. Clean it well and then set it out to dry in the Sun for a few days.

To make blessed water, gather a jarful from a nearby river or creek. To bless it, recite 2 Corinthians 9:8 while placing your right hand above the bowl of water. As an animistic prayer, you may recite one I have written:

By spirits of the land and sky,
By spirits of the mountains and rivers,
By every tree and stone gathered here,
May blessings be bestowed upon this water,
For today, tomorrow, and forevermore.

With the thread, cut enough to cover most of the wishbone if you were to wrap it around and around. Dip the thread into the blessed water, and allow it to dry.

Once both the wishbone and thread are dry, begin the working by honing in on the wish you'd like granted. Is there anything that you could use a little extra support in? This could be increasing financial means or luck in your career path. Focus and hold the image tightly in your mental grip.

Take the red thread and tie a knot at one end of the wishbone. Then, twist the thread around the wishbone. Allow this to be a slow movement and remain entirely focused on the desired wish. Twist the length of the thread until the wishbone is fully covered, tying a knot at the other end to complete the work.

Fumigate the charm with an herbal incense blend of mint and chamomile. Both are used magically to attract good luck. Place the enchanted charm at your work desk, in a personal bag, or where you are most present for your desired wish.

MOUNTAIN FOLK ART

Culture is not created in solitude but in togetherness. The diverse landscape and people of Appalachia created a unique library of artistry and craftsmanship. What we see preserved today as mountain folk art is the creative pursuits born out of necessity. In these isolated, rugged landscapes, survival depended on cunning ways. Crafts were made from all-natural materials with detailed skill and patience. Most folk art wasn't designed with selling in mind. Instead, these goods were designed to meet a specific need. Handcrafted items hardly ever left the original maker's possession unless passed down to a relative or gifted as a family heirloom. This is how we can distinguish folk art from modernized fine art. When roads and highways were built leading into small mountain towns, the artistry of locals became more exposed. It became an attraction for those not from the area who grew an appreciation of the unique regional artwork.

Appalachian folk art has evolved over time, and its preservation has become a sacred endeavor to grasp a hold of the past. During the 19th and 20th centuries, the revival of Appalachian folk arts was pioneered by individuals and organizations committed to recording this craft before it was forgotten. Among the early folklorists were John C. Campbell and Olive Dame Campbell, whose mission was not religious in nature but rather one of cultural preservation. The Campbells were captivated by the Appalachian region. Through their fieldwork, they began documenting the various forms of art, music, and oral traditions, as well as collaborating with other folklorists on such assignments. This work contributed significantly to the collections found in archives and libraries to explore the Appalachian craftsmanship and culture. It laid the foundation for a broader movement to preserve the region's arts and crafts with organizations and institutions with the shared goal. One such institution is the John C. Campbell Folk School in North Carolina, where a variety of courses are offered focusing on Appalachian folk music and traditional arts. It is a chance for individuals to learn, practice, and preserve some of the region's traditions.

The Campbells' work was only the beginning and can be viewed with some speculation since their perspective focused solely on the region's European influence. Observing only the Campbells' work leaves out the remainder of the diverse story written. There were many hands involved in shaping clay, weaving the threads, and strumming strings. To focus solely on the British Isles influence is to see only a sliver of the full painted picture. As a result, several other figures and organizations took it upon themselves to highlight the multicultural present voices. Alan Lomax, for example, was a songcatcher and collected music and stories from the southern hills. He took special notice of how songs crossed between cultures and were import-ant for the working class in his fieldwork. Other folklorists picked up the assignment to identify African American origins, such as John Wesley Work III, who recorded various collections of African-rooted folk songs.

I share this list in hopes of inspiring an appreciation for folk arts and how they can be applied in a magical act, often referred to as *hearthcraft*. Hearthcraft is a modern term that focuses on creating magical moments in the mundane and commonly involves the art of handcrafting. When I began incorporating new rituals in my practice, I found that crafting was a way to alchemize my emotions and create physical representations of inten-tional spells.

Who knew that my tears could be used in a watercolor painting? With each brush stroke and my heart openly present, grief turned into healing art. Or that the fire of my justified anger could propel my sewing needle? Every stitch held the frustration of disappointments so that my heart could let them go. Or how peace would allow me to connect with intuition as I morphed wet clay into an offering vessel? Each item an imprint of the magic created by my own two hands.

Woodcarving

Prior to the lumber extraction companies' intrusion, there was an abundance of trees in Appalachia. The dense forests provided ideal material for tools like the wagon, but our ancestors were not limited to crafting just labor tools. They also carved home wares such as kitchen utensils, as well as kids' toys. Some folks used woodcarving to craft replicas of religious figures as a representation of their faith.

Others had crafted furniture such as tables and chairs. Chairs especially became a significant art form post–Civil War. New and improved styles emerged, such as the "settin' chair," coined by Birdie Mace from North Carolina. This Appalachian chair was inspired by the New England style chair that was made with comfort in mind, creating a supportive back with laddered slats. But the rocking chair became a signature. Family members would craft them as gifts for front porches to sit and soak up the morning light. Sometimes they'd be gifts for expecting relatives to help soothe a baby to sleep before bed. Eventually, furniture such as the rocking chair became manufactured, but it never meant as much as the one handcrafted and handed down by a relative.

Today, woodcarving can be done for both practicality and for pleasure. I've got a few acquaintances who have a very fine hand at crafting wooden spoons with intricate details of flora on the handle. For practitioners who include cooking and baking as part of their craft, a handmade wooden spoon can be a tool to use in transferring intentional energy from themselves to the meal. Likewise, wooden hairbrushes can be carved with protective symbols and used to cleanse away evil eye when brushing the hair.

Textile Weaving

Weaving was yet another form of artistry that can be done for multiple purposes, such as household items, bedding, and clothing. Sheep were a viable resource for folks as they could harvest the wool for these textile needs. Sheep were quite easy to manage as farm animals with their low-maintenance care—aside from their thick wool. They wouldn't wander too far from the property unless something startled them, making them great homestead companions. Out in the forest, they'd forage for most of the day, fending for themselves, but they always returned home for a safe place to rest and recover before going back out again.

Once it was time, folks would shear the sheep and prepare the wool for carding and spinning. Spindles were used to spin the wool into thread onto a bobbin to make yarns for clothing, bedding, and other textiles. Weaving was a popular art form done by most of the Appalachian women. For generations, they were responsible for making the household's clothing and blankets by hand, before mass production of textiles and machinery simplified the process.

They'd naturally dye the material to customize the yarn coloring from sheep's wool. Walnut bark was dug up from the roots to boil, resulting in a rich brown pigment. Gray moss from an apple tree was used to dye for an orange-yellow tone, as was broom straw. Through a magical practitioner's lens, this approach is another way to work with a specific plant spirit. Working alongside plants can be quite fruitful, and there is no better person who understands the energy plants transmit than Appalachian folks. By naturally dying fabric with a specific plant, the fabric is infused with the plant's energy.

Today, fiber arts encompass a wide range of creative expressions, from hand sewing our own garments to needling a child's wool felt toy. The rhythm that comes from the movement helps us enter a trance state, where our focus is solely on the motion and purpose of the workpiece. With each intentional knot made, a desire is captured in time. The result is a physical representation of such spoken requests, like a scarf enchanted for the recipient to feel attractive and loved while wearing it.

Quilting and Needlework

The art of quilting was deeply appreciated for its multifaceted significance. Quilting served a practical purpose beyond just passing the time, as many crafts did. It wasn't just about creating a blanket for warmth. These authentic handmade quilts became physical representations of familial tales and community historical narratives.

Patchwork quilting, popularized in the 17th century, is the form of quilting many are most familiar with. This approach involves working with a variety of fabrics in different colors and making various quilting blocks to stitch together an intricate pattern. Some quilters would use leftover scraps of old clothing from relatives to stitch together a quilt that represented each family member. In the close-knit communities of quilt guilds, folks would come together to create large detailed quilts by hand. The quilt in progress would be displayed on a table with everyone gathered around a designated section for hand-stitching. This craft was locally cherished and served as a bond between many friendships.

Quilting went beyond being just a physical representation of a family member's love and became a way of discreetly making political statements during the Civil War era. Specific quilting patterns and blocks were shaped by these notable moments. Quilts would be made to represent a family's solidarity with the soldiers on either side. They became popular items to be sold at fairs to help raise funds for their men at war.

Some quilt blocks were believed to carry encoded messages, often referenced as Underground Railroad quilts. Symbols such as log cabins and animals were meticulously sewn into the quilted design and then displayed coincidentally outside—a silent language communicating with enslaved men, women, and children seeking safety from the Deep South. While historians may not have unearthed concrete evidence of this secret code within the quilting world, that does not void the belief of its existence among people who believed safety often meant secrecy, too. It is then understandable that tangible, physical evidence may be elusive. These artifacts are described in Jacqueline L. Tobin and Raymond G. Dobard's *Hidden in Plain View: A Secret Story of Quilts and the Underground Railroad*.

This needlecraft style remains a cherished tradition today. It is yet another opportunity where knot magic can be applied. Every piece of fabric and tool has its own spirit. The practitioner can work with them to weave magic with their needle and thread. The metal of the needle is associated with strength, durability, and transformation. A stitching spell has become my chosen way to craft magical goods for myself, my beloved friends, and my community. Every quilted piece is sewn with love, patience, and purpose with the support of my guiding spirits.

Basketweaving

Basketweaving art forms originate specifically from the Cherokee here. As this art form grew, each maker introduced specific weaving patterns and materials significant to their tradition. These handcrafted baskets were sturdy enough to use for foraging wild berries, nuts, and other plants for apothecary and cooking needs. They were customized for what was needed in a self-sufficient world: egg baskets, market baskets, flower baskets . . . the list is endless.

The natural materials that were used to handcraft these baskets vary, but some local favorites are white oak, honeysuckle vines, corn husks, and willow bark. The shape and pattern would vary from what was generationally taught. A popular Appalachian style that sits in the Smithsonian American Art Museum is a representation of the gizzard basket. The unique shape was created with the intent that the basket would rest on one's hip while traveling to protect the fragile delicacies gathered within. The basket was woven with hand-split white oak and is just one of the many examples of the unique patterns of Appalachian baskets.

Pottery

The trees provided lumber for woodcarving, the sheep provided wool for yarn, and the vines provided rope for baskets; but the earth provided an older tradition before the New World, and that's the art of pottery. The magic of working with the clay beneath our feet can be traced back to the Cherokee, Catawba, and Choctaw communities, where clay was rich around the nearby rivers. They collected clay to craft themselves vessels to be used for practicality and spirituality.

The bowls would be carved with symbols and patterns that told the story of resilience and strength, the enduring spirit of the mountains and home. The arrival of Europeans brought additional methods of pottery making, yet again joining the two methods to create an authentic Appalachian folk art, birthed from the earth itself and representing a deep connection to the land.

The clay used for the pottery pieces also has its own personality and character. In the Carolinas, red clay was well sought after for its rich terra-cotta tone. I remember being a young kid playing at my grandparents' cabin where they had bare red clay spots across the yard. I was in awe of the scarlet color. It reminded me of Mars. Mostly, clay can be gathered around riverbanks and preserved for working into a vessel of your choosing. It is a wonderful way to work with the spirit of soil.

FROM MAMAW'S BOOK OF SPELLS:
Quilted Charm Bag

Growing up as the daughter and granddaughter of a quilter and seamstress might suggest that stitch crafting skills would come naturally to me. However, it has been a learning process with its own set of challenges, one that has taught me many lessons. The intricate detail involved is truly remarkable, and through continued practice, I have come to appreciate the virtue of patience.

Sitting at my wooden desk with bits of thread, several pairs of scissors, and fabric scraps (often the result of cutting errors), it may appear chaotic to an outsider. Yet, it represents the intense focus of a desired intent: the image of an art piece vivid in my mind that was inspired by an intention ready to take its physical form. The crafting offers a quiet moment that I find myself needing on some days more than others.

Among the various forms of sewing quilts, I've particularly embraced the appliqué method, especially when crafting discreet charm bags for the home or friends. To an ordinary viewer, these quaint fabric pillows may seem like nothing more; but for me, they hold a subtle magic.

To create your own quilted charm bag, begin by gathering these materials:

- Blessed water

- Dried juniper

- Matches or a lighter

- A charcoal disk and tray

- A sewing needle

- Thread to match your fabric

- A 6x6-inch fabric square of your choosing

- Scissors

- Organic cotton fill

- Pins (optional)

To begin our magical crafting, we will call on our Appalachian matriarchs who are knowledgeable in this craft to guide our work.

Gather your materials and lay them to the left of your fireproof container with the dried juniper. Begin by washing your hands with the blessed water and pat dry to cleanse any stagnant energy. Burn the dried juniper on a charcoal disk in the fireproof container. As the juniper burns, close your eyes and recite the following prayer: "I call upon the spirits of my matriarchs who threaded their needles and sewed their stitches. Guide my hand and bless my tools for the work done today. Hear my prayer with every stitch, and let it be carried out forevermore."

Open your eyes. With your thread, pass through the juniper smoke and then place it on the right-hand side. With your needle, pass it through the juniper smoke and then place it on the right-hand side. With your fabric, pass it through the juniper smoke and then place it on the right-hand side.

You are now ready to sew your charm bag.

Fold your fabric square in half with the right sides facing each other. Press gently to create a crease along the fold. Thread your needle, and then knot the end of your thread to secure it. Starting at one corner close to the folded edge, begin sewing along the open edges of the fabric square. Use a running stitch or backstitch, leaving a small seam allowance (about ¼ inch). Continue sewing along the sides, leaving one side open enough to fill. Ensure your stitches are secure.

Carefully turn the fabric bag inside out so that the right sides are now facing outward. Fill the bag with the organic cotton fill and any corresponding dried herbs for your desired intention. Fold the raw edges of the open seam inward to create a neat edge. Thread your needle again and sew along the remaining open side using a neat running stitch or whip stitch. Ensure to securely close the opening. Trim any excess thread and inspect the bag for any loose stitches.

If you'd like, you can play around with wool appliqué on the fabric square prior to sewing the fabric together. For example, I will cut out a heart or house shape to represent a loving home. The design is inspired by the intent. Position the wool on your fabric, pin it so that it stays in place, then blanket-stitch the shape with your needle and thread. You can also incorporate other embroidery protection symbols.

SONGCATCHERS AND BALLADS

Food may be the heart of the southern highlander, but music is the soul. Heartfelt ballads and songs were inspired by historical moments during some of the region's darkest times. Not every song was solemn, however. They were also lively and used for entertainment. The stories told through song were exaggerations for the sake of having a good tale to share. Local folk would sing their choruses for fun, to pass the time during hard labor, to grieve and process, to pray to their Lord, or to soothe children with lullabies and bedtime stories.

Those who migrated to the southern hills never forgot their homelands. The old ballads spoke to the nostalgia of walking the unbeaten path, fighting for freedom, celebrating a resilient spirit, and navigating the complex emotions of starting a new life far from home. The songs were sung with sentimentality and unwavering pride. The rough terrain matched their rough spirits, and the mountaineers combatted any underlying fear of settling into unfamiliar territory.

The region may have been perceived as lagging compared to other communities, but on the contrary this allowed for traditions like songs to endure. Historians and folklorists became interested in preserving the region's music and tracing back its origins, finding related chords, lyrics, and tempos that corresponded to those from abroad. Those who pursued these regional songs were known as songcatchers.

The first noteworthy songcatchers that began this recordkeeping were English folklorist Cecil Sharp and his assistant Maud Karpeles. Sharp met the Campbells in the early 20th century and began exploring the Appalachian region in hopes of capturing the fleeting, rich music. Sharp and Karpeles took on the assignment of exploring counties in southern Appalachia to not only record locals singing their ballads but also to identify similarities to songs across the British Isles.

In their work, they recorded a large collection of songs and ballads that made their way overseas. However, it is worth noting that their work focused solely on retrieving ties to British influence, leaving out the full picture of the region's musical scene. Their work can help verify that some songs of the working class from the British Isles made their way over, but to conclude that they were of their purest form is almost impossible. These local songs were influenced by those who shared them with others, crossing over between class and race. Therefore, in order to capture the truest vibrancy of the ballads and songs of Appalachia, observing the work of folklorist Alan Lomax introduces such a collection. Lomax understood that there was more to the story and took on the assignment of unveiling the true colors of American folk songs, with its diverse storyline that pays homage to its history.

Music became an integral part of everyday life. It unified the people. It puts words and tunes to life's ebbs and flows of loss and love, hardship and strength, unity and loneliness. A favored folk song that my father often strummed on his guitar, especially after the release of the film *O Brother, Where Art Thou?* was "Down to the River to Pray." This song echoes the southern region's religious practices. The earliest version, "The Good Old Way," was published in *Slave Songs of the United States* in 1867 and contributed by George H. Allan of Nashville, Tennessee. The lyrics are as follows:

As I went down in the valley to pray,
Studying about that good old way,
When you shall wear the starry crown,
Good Lord, show me the way.
O mourner, let's go down, let's go down, let's go down,
O mourner, let's go down,
Down in the valley to pray

This popular folk song was commonly sung in churches or during baptisms. I recall the song being recited during one of my attended church sermons as a child. The lyrics reference the purification and cleansing rituals of Baptists that are performed in local rivers, a marking of a new chapter where individuals devote themselves to the Lord's guidance.

Some of the region's songs reflected significant historical moments. During the Mine Wars, songs were composed to be sung in unison, uniting miners in the face of corporate corruption. A miner poem-turned-song collected in the *United Mine Workers Journal* in May 1895 speaks of these trying times. Recorded by Isaac Hanna of Englewood, Illinois, the song became known as "The Company Store" and went as follows:

The lot of the miner,
At best is quite hard,
We work for good money,
Get paid with a card;
We scarcely can live,
And not a cent more,
Since we're paid off in checks
On the company store.

Those great coal monopolies
Are growing apace,
They are making their millions
By grinding our face;
Unto their high prices
The people pay toll,
While they pay fifty cents
For mining their coal.

They keep cutting our wages
Time after time,
Where we once had a dollar,
We now have a dime;
While our souls are near famished,
And our bodies are sore,

We are paid off in checks,

On the company store.

Additionally, murder ballads were told for some good ole entertainment. One enduring murder ballad that has translated over time and land is "The Twa Sisters," known by various names over time, including "The Cruel Sister" and "The Bonnie Swans." This ballad, though shortened over time, tells the story of two sisters who fight for the affection of a young knight. Ultimately, the knight chooses the "young and fair" sister. In a fit of jealousy, the older sister lures the younger one to a creek and pushes her into the water. The young sister drowns, and a local miller discovers her body. According to some versions, the miller uses her body and hair to create a stringed instrument, such as a harp or fiddle. At the wedding of the knight and the older sister, the instrument "sings" the ballad of the younger sister's death, revealing the older sister's treachery.

The fiddle, often regarded as the favored instrument of the mountaineer, had made its travel overseas along the migration path of the Old World. Its size made it an ideal traveling companion, eventually integrating into the music scene of southern Appalachia. The fiddle became a staple for quick-tempo melodies performed at weddings, parties, hearthside gatherings, and even funerals.

Other stringed instruments rose in the music scene when various cultures influenced one another. The banjo comes to the forefront. My father had one, though he hardly played it. The African-inspired banjo entered the scene post–Civil War in the 19th century. Later, the dulcimer, with its Germanic roots. Then, the string guitar and mandolin came into the picture. An orchestra of stringed instruments became available to the landscape for the folk musician to choose to their liking. It would become another generational skill set passed down from one to the next.

The discovery of Appalachian musical talent launched during the early 20th century with the popularization of the radio, forever altering the musical landscape. Audiences nationwide were captivated by country tunes of Appalachia. The novel music transported them to a world unlike their own, all from the comfort of their homes. This genre's nationalization continued to expand, branching into subgenres such as bluegrass, whose popularity soared with Bill Monroe's banjo and its haunting "lonesome sound" in the 1930s.

Some of the country's most iconic musicians, performers, and songwriters were born and raised in Appalachia. Loretta Lynn is a familiar Southern household name when scanning the landscape. Lynn's songs resonate with those of Kentucky roots. Her songs speak on the intricacies of growing up as a coal miner's daughter—in fact, "Coal Miner's Daughter" would later become one of her most famous songs. Bessie Smith from Tennessee became an icon in the bluegrass genre as one of the first Black singers to be recorded. We are also blessed with other musical talents, such as Dolly Parton, another familiar household name. She continues to be a beacon of light within the mountain region with her kind spirit. She doesn't take her platform for granted. She has advocated for essential topics in the area like access to education and health in her home state of Tennessee and other parts of Appalachia.

The 1960s folk music revival played a crucial role in preserving and revitalizing mountain music's future. Musicians of all backgrounds eagerly sought to recreate porch performances, accompanied by the timeless melodies of banjos and fiddles. The years of admiration and rejuvenation have inspired current festivals across the southern region that are happening today, such as the Appalachian Folk Festival in Brevard, North Carolina, ensuring that the heritage of mountain music continues to be celebrated and connecting new generations with their cultural roots.

MOUNTAIN FAITH

Faith is unique in southern Appalachia. It is not strictly one thing over the other, but a blend creating something uniquely diverse. Religion served as a guiding light and reason for the early mountaineers. While the British Isles immigrants brought Protestant traditions, Germanic immigrants brought their Catholic traditions, and Eastern Europeans brought their Eastern Orthodox traditions. Though their prayers and churches may have varied, the purpose remained the same: to build a meaningful, spiritual connection with the Christian God. The Christian God goes by many names here. The Lord. The Savior. The Creator. The Holy Spirit. The Holy Trinity of the Father, Son, and Holy Ghost. How I was raised was to reference this entity as the Lord, so I will do so moving forward.

The influence of Christianity can be found in the region's traditional healing and doctoring practices, but some practitioners didn't fully adopt the doctrine. On the contrary, animistic beliefs that predated Christianity were not entirely left behind. A deep reverence and shared value of living in harmony with the natural world remained central for many. The mountain landscape is a living, breathing spirit that inspires its residents with holy hilltops. Practitioners aligned their rituals and seasonal holiday observances with the rhythms of the land, praying to figures and folkloric spirits. This spiritual connection between the practitioner, the land, and their Lord established a dual religion—a belief I like to refer to as *mountain faith*, where Christianity and animism meet. This perspective is inspired by the sentiment that the land is a blessed creation by the Lord described in the book of Genesis. Similarly outside of this structured religion, animism recognizes the land as an honorable spirit. This faith adapts and twists in the working hands, becoming a guided force of purpose.

Within the mountain faith, the church became a central part of the early mountaineers' lives. Weekly attendance at the local church dressed in Sunday best attire was part of community participation. Even those not originally part of structured religions joined churches, influenced by their kin to partake in community norms. Attendance was seen as a neighborly duty, with nonattendance sometimes raising an eyebrow of suspicion, especially during periods when accusations of witchcraft posed a threat and could lead to church trials.

Having grown up in a Southern Baptist household, I am most familiar with their teachings, which emphasize direct communication with the Lord. Baptists are known for their humility in prayer, thanking the Lord for the simplest of necessities like a roof over their head and food on their table. "Oh, thank the Lord!" was a common household remark, whether it was purposeful or not. Not a single blessing wasn't accounted for during morning prayer or over supper. They are humble in their personal connection to the Lord. I had visited other churches to observe several practices like Catholic and Pentecostal. What I discovered was the varying ways folks communicate with the Lord. Growing up in a Baptist household, I was taught that anything could be done through prayer. Should a neighbor need healing, say a prayer. Should we need a little extra financial support, say a prayer. Prayer was the main form of communication to modestly speak our needs while giving thanks for daily blessings.

Understanding the early mountaineer's faith provides context for why prayers were recited in healing traditions and how the modern folk practitioner might decide to incorporate such verses. The Bible was a main source for guiding the practitioner's work. Missionaries who visited the southern mountains in the 19th century introduced the King James Version (KJV) of the Bible, leading to many Southern churches favoring it for their sermons. It is the version that I reference in my own work. My childhood copy sits on my working desk with old handwritten notes from my early study days. I incorporate the Bible in my work as a way to venerate my ancestors' tradition, but with a heretical approach. I reference traditional verses to rewrite prayers that address my animistic interpretation of Spirit or other spirits that fit the working or petition. You will see some of these alternative prayers throughout this book in addition to what is traditionally used for your own discretion. It's important to note that the Bible held great significance for the southern region, and healers, conjurers, and other practitioners of all kinds referenced it often. Verses from this text are also found in notable folk magic books such as John George Hohman's *Long Lost Friend*. It's said that Southern Christians believed more intensely than any group outside the South, and I think that speaks volumes as to why we see such strong mountain faith in our early Appalachian traditions.

Folk Saints and Figures

The Appalachian practitioner may seek guidance from spirits like folk saints in their work. For example, a practitioner who had grown up within a Catholic household might feel a pull to a specific saint that their family members had petitioned, even if they don't adhere to the Christian doctrine. If the saint is significant to their family or culture, the practitioner may petition this spirit for a current need such as support, protection, or guidance. In other approaches, such as for Baptists, saints are not necessarily intermediaries between the petitioner and the Lord. Instead, they are regarded as equals to those who demonstrate faithful living, which many strived to achieve in their devotions.

To me, folk saints are representations of certain qualities or ideals that resonate with the human experience. They personify nature and are archetypes venerated for desires that align with their attributes. They also carry cultural significance as respected, symbolic spirits that can be petitioned when people find themselves in need.

There are a few folk saints that come to the forefront of my mind. John the Baptist is a figure I grew up learning about in my Bible studies. His stories involved baptizing folks who sought to cleanse themselves of their old life to enter the new one and walk alongside their Lord. For this reason, his spirit can be petitioned for cleansing and purification workings, as well as offering a guiding light for those who feel lost. Saint Mary is a familiar cross-cultural figure who goes by different names depending on the specific context. She is petitioned by those seeking maternal guidance and protection. Her image alone offers strong protection and healing, with her picture used as a charm for safety. She is called upon for support in family matters and creating harmony within the home.

Petitioning a folk saint or other figure often reflects where we're at personally in our lives. Having grown up in a Baptist household, it never occurred to me to petition saints until I entered a difficult period in my life. A friend recommended that I pray to Saint Michael to cure a broken heart. I created a small altar on my bedside table with a photo of Saint Michael and a blessed candle, and recited a healing prayer for seven consecutive days. One evening, as I spoke the prayer with deep reverence, I felt this overwhelming presence that brought tears to my eyes and relief in my chest. I hold that experience close, as it significantly supported my healing journey.

Additionally, practitioners may feel called to petition figures that are significant to their ancestral indigenous and diaspora practices that predate Christianity. For example, when I began a new chapter of my path, I felt drawn to the figure Brigid. Folklorists have been bridging stories to make conclusions that perhaps Brigid is closely associated with Saint Brigid of Kildare after Ireland adopted Catholicism. When Christianity reached Ireland, many deities were absorbed into new roles, while some were completely excluded. Brigid's regional Irish folklore speaks to the many aspects of her identity. Her spirit may be petitioned for matters of the home, healing, poetry, alchemy, and craftsmanship. While exploring her full story goes beyond this discussion, I mention her name with fondness as she remains an important figure in my practice today.

There's also recognition of local saints. Local saints refer to popular individuals within a community whose lives represent a theme of importance, such as grace, justice, or generosity. This individual's spirit is honored for the life they lived that created a ripple effect, leaving a lasting impression on the community. An example would be a local hero, or someone who advocated for great change.

Mountain Faith Rituals

The mountain faith has many spiritual rituals that were intended to bring the believer closer to the Lord. Some of these rituals would include water to cleanse the soul. It is a dedication to their faith, to be "born again," and reassurance that they are blessed for eternity. These rituals mirror some older traditions of cleansing with water. Baptisms are most common in Southern churches. They were large community gatherings rather than a singular rite between you and the Lord.

A powerful image I found of my great-Papaw was his baptism in Pike County. The black-and-white image that had clearly been scanned to upload onto the family tree had a deep crease in the middle of it, as if it had been stored in someone's pocket for safekeeping. My Papaw is standing in the middle of the river with a bridge ahead full of people sitting and standing around him. He stands with his arms across his chest in preparation to be dunked into the river by the pastor standing beside him.

In a way, this ritual is like a funeral. Not like the kind where your body is buried under the soil marked by a gravestone. The kind of funeral where your body is immersed in water and then lifted back up again. *You are reborn!* they'd holler in the distance, clapping and congratulating you as you waded back to land. Your past life before walking into the river now washed away as you entered a new one devoted to faith. The deepest of cleansings. A new start.

Foot washing is another ritual that is practiced in some Southern churches. It is a humbling experience. First of all, you have to be comfortable with touching another person's feet. Second, you must be okay with someone touching your feet. This ritual is referenced in John 13:4–15 where Jesus is cleansing the feet of each of his disciples. The concept of washing the individual's spirit is also applied in this ritual and is sometimes done in replacement of a baptism if the church doesn't have access to a large enough body of water or bathtub. This rite can be performed outside this doctrine. Cleansing one's feet with a foot wash can open doors when we're feeling lost. I like to use warm water, Epsom salt, and a black tea-bag. Make your foot bath and recite over the concoction: "May what hinders my path be cleansed and restored by the guidance of my wise and well ancestors."

Other rituals included sermons that evoked the Lord to become overwhelmed with the holy presence. As the pastor spoke with power and devotion, the room would fill with intense emotions. The attendee would relax into a trancelike state of mind, completely letting go of expectations and focusing only on the words spoken, allowing themselves to be overtaken by worship. Hands would be raised above their heads, some would feel called to dance, and others would begin speaking in tongues. I've witnessed these worshippers before, once when a friend invited me to her Pentecostal church. There wasn't anything like that in the churches I grew up going to. At one point in the sermon, everyone was speaking a language I had never heard in unison, guided by the pastor while looking and pointing to the left side of the room. It was an experience that I won't ever forget.

COMMUNING WITH THE LAND

Communing with the land is another cornerstone of mountain faith, where the environment is not just a background. Animism in Appalachia isn't just a way of seeing the world; it's a way of participating in it. It's a mindset and view that everything has a spirit, a living essence that deserves mutual respect and can accept participation in the practitioner's work. This perspective is one of the oldest beliefs across various traditions.

Here in Appalachia, animism draws inspiration from the spirituality of Indigenous Peoples, as well as older practices that predated Christianity. I have been in conversations with local practitioners about the revival of animism in many modern practices. It may not have been widely discussed before in these mountains, but it is a belief that many do share. To the mountain folk, everything around is alive and has its own energy, forming a vibrant ecosystem of spiritual allies. There is magic in the listening. Animism roots the practitioner's heart, allowing them to see that all parts of the natural world carry a special kind of wisdom.

This relationship with nature isn't passive—it's a reciprocal bond, like the ones with our neighbors and other spirits. An interconnectedness that we are not separate from nature, but instead part of it. When speaking about these spirits, it is similar to the way that we speak to one another. The local river I visit is a spirit that has helped me move things along when areas of my life have felt stagnant. While wading in the river, allowing the water to flow around me, I have fed it my concerns. In exchange, I bring a bag to collect the litter that mindless people have left behind. Some days, I sing to the water. This relationship has helped remove old narratives that left me stagnant. I simply wash them down the river, letting them go freely.

DOWN THE RABBIT HOLE
Civil War Quilts

My aunt loaned me one of her favorite books on Civil War quilts. In the book is listed and pictured a variety of quilting blocks that became popular during the Civil War era. Hence, why they're called Civil War quilts. The fabric designs are simple. They're the ones I am most drawn to today, displaying intricate details of shapes like flowers, triangles, dots, and more. What I found most interesting in this book is the history behind the many quilting blocks that quilters use to weave their stories into the fabrics.

One in particular that I've been most drawn to is the Ohio Star. It goes by other names such as Star of Ohio, Sawtooth Star, Eight-Pointed Star, or Lone Star. The design is one of the easier ones for beginners to make. It consists of a single square in the center with half-square triangles and square patches to create an eight-pointed star. The half-square triangles are positioned to surround the center square to make the star formation. The chosen color palette can play a role in creating many different versions using this simple pattern.

When I looked further into how this specific star became so popular, I discovered its 19th-century story. In Oberlin, Ohio, is the esteemed liberal arts school Oberlin College. It was one of the first colleges to admit women and African American students. This college attracted a young Black man named Lewis Sheridan Leary, who relocated from Fayetteville, North Carolina. During his time there, he met an antislavery advocate by the name of John Brown. Brown was determined to get together a group of men to help him on his mission of taking over Harpers Ferry, a federal armory in West Virginia. Leary was one of the men recruited on this mission to incite the end of slavery. Though the men did not succeed, as they were either captured or killed, it did cause national disruption to begin the overall movement that led to the Civil War between the North and South.

Leary's wife, Mary, learned of his passing when she was handed a shirt she had made him riddled with bullet holes. It is known that Mary was the one who sewed the Ohio Star while sitting on the porch with her kids. It now stands as a quilt block that reminds many of Leary's brave story.

3

BY THE DEVIL'S HAND: WITCHERY IN SOUTHERN APPALACHIA

My spiritual journey was guided by the rhododendron pathways of the Blue Ridge Mountains. Although my parents dedicated me before the church and I attended a private school that required memorization of Bible verses, they were still open-minded to matters of spirituality and religion.

The teachings I learned at school and church had an undertone of fear and conservative values that didn't align with my heart. I was taught to love my neighbor, and yet the teachings I heard sometimes contradicted that philosophy. While the freedom to decipher my own beliefs was unfamiliar ground, I nonetheless decided to explore other beliefs and interpretations of God. Not necessarily the Christian God, but divinity in some other sense. In these waking moments, I recognized the breath of weeping willows, backyard creeks, and open fields, and retreated to mountaintops that would become my new church.

I discovered that my spirituality is rooted in animism with a witchcraft practice. (I can just feel some of my ancestors rolling in their graves right now!) I had taken a special interest in reading early records of witches, and it became apparent that there were power struggles between those within the church and those who paved their own path. If one questioned the mountain pastor's teachings, false accusations of dealing with the devil were projected. Discretion was then practiced by those who revered older spirits to keep their identity under wraps. That same fearful undertone still exists in some parts here. The idea of someone labeling themselves a witch or practicing witchcraft often evokes a sense of unfamiliarity from others. "What do you mean?" they'll ask.

A common thread between historical and local records of witchcraft was the devil's presence. The figure is tethered to unlocking what is hidden and granting magical knowledge that was described as forbidden. His reputation isn't favored in Appalachia. "You've got the devil in ya" or "dancing with the devil" are all catchphrases that encompass that he's to blame for wrongful doings—though "wrongful" could be up for debate, depending on the specific circumstance. I found this narrative from across the pond repeated in our mountains here, that the devil's involvement insinuated you were up to no good. But who is this devil . . . and who is he not? And why were defiant, justified acts in the name of protecting oneself or another concluded to be the work of the devil?

Walking this path required dismantling the inherited view of the Christian God, a god who punished deviation from rules taught by man. By deconstructing this doctrine, I came to understand Spirit as a connection—Spirit is me, and I am Spirit, as are my neighbors and the earth I commune with—uniquely shaped by my relationship with the spiritual ecosystem and divinity rather than a dogma. Despite what some of my Appalachian ancestors may have considered as "blasphemy," it gives me a sense of liberation. To walk the crooked path is to embrace complexity, to live as an embodiment of liminality.

Before delving into the witch lore of Appalachia, it's important to first acknowledge the historical roots of *witchcraft*. Before Christianity became the dominant religion, there were various forms of older spiritual practices. These beliefs were not viewed as sinister or deviant, but rather as essential components of spiritual and healing traditions. They were inspired by people's profound connection with nature. Witchcraft, according to early records, involved specific regional beliefs, nature worship, and the veneration of multiple figures. This worldview was rooted in the rhythms of the land and celebrated the cycle of life with regional traditions that were an accepted part of cultural life.

The records we have of these practices date back to the earliest manuscripts recovered from European sources, with some traces stretching as far back as the pre-Christian era, though documentation becomes more frequent in the 15th century. Despite the limited physical evidence, it's clear that these spiritual practices were an integral part of cultural customs. With the rise of Christianity, they were syncretized into the new religious framework. The new monotheistic faith not only rejected the polytheistic beliefs but actively sought to demonize them. What had once been ordinary folk practices began to be labeled as heretical, and those who continued to engage in them were increasingly seen as dangerous.

Literature published by two inquisitors of the Catholic Church known as *Malleus Maleficarum* became a key instrument in the systematic persecution. It accused individuals of practicing what they defined as *witchcraft*, which referenced spiritual practices described as anything but the monotheistic religion of Christianity. It portrayed witchcraft as a form of heresy, equating it with Devil worship and framing witches as a threat to both Christian society and the moral order. The shift in perception turned what had once been culturally shared spiritual practices into harmful acts to others through supernatural means. Practices rooted in animism were no longer seen as an expression of spirituality tied to the natural world but as a grave sin, a danger to Christian communities, and something to be eradicated.

As Christianity spread and solidified its power across Europe, the fear of witches grew, culminating in widespread witch hunts and trials. Local communities, driven by fear and religious fervor, took matters into their own hands. They began accusing neighbors of witchcraft, which often led to horrific executions of many innocent people. The term *witch* became synonymous with something of evil nature, forever altering the public perception of these ancient practices.

Historic court hearings reveal community members accusing individuals as suspected witches. In these recordings, the accused would either plead innocent or confess to meeting with the devil to renounce their Christian faith. While describing in detail their encounter, they mentioned partaking in some kind of initiation rite. This would involve placing one hand on their head and the other on their foot, claiming that the entirety of their body belonged to the devil. They allowed the devil to bite them, leaving a mark, and used their own shed blood to sign his contractual book. Additionally, records describe them meeting with the devil at night, traveling by broom to steal from their enemies' homes, or gathering with others who made their own deal with the devil.

It is described that if a cunning practitioner provided magical solutions to an inquiring client that led to a negative experience, accusations would begin to arise that they were not a healer—but a witch! The list of workings in these historical accounts includes a series of charms that were created by the local healer or conjurer. Many accusations were made under false pretenses by petty neighbors seeking personal vengeance. During this time period—a horrific historical era—these recorded accusations led to the belief that witches were associated with specific plants, the folkloric devil, rites, and the otherworld. These associations inspired the stories brought over into Appalachia about witchcraft are still linked to and inspire modern traditional witchcraft practices.

By the colonial period, witch hunts began to subside, although, people still acknowledged the witch's presence in whispered tones. When European settlers arrived, they brought along their preconceived notions of witchcraft and biases against unfamiliar spiritual practices that were not of their own Christian religion. The speculated fear of witchcraft had crossed the Atlantic. By Appalachia's definition, witches were identified as those who lived alone, had no claimed religion, had certain physical features and markings, had the ability to shapeshift into animals, or engaged with spirits and figures outside the Christian framework. With Christianity becoming the dominant religion, witchcraft had to adapt—as it always does. The isolated southern Appalachian region allowed for the preservation and evolution of such otherworldly magic, which granted fertile soil for its revival under a new identity. Practitioners who kept their methods a secret taught the next generation, who would then teach their own one day under a slightly different identity.

The conversation of witchcraft in the southern mountain region lies in the paradox of something old and something new. Individuals who partook in such magical practices prior to the 20th century would have never used the term *witch* to describe themselves and their craft, as many of them had converted to Christianity and refrained from any association with the devil. Nonetheless, the devil's presence was still acknowledged as a gatekeeper of the witch's path. Practitioners and witches alike firmly believed that divine work was at hand in their magical practice. This divine influence was attributed to various sources—God, saints, ancestors, the devil, or another spirit of the land. What remained consistent across beliefs is a deep faith that something or someone was supporting the work done by the practitioner's hands and spoken words. With this knowledge, they could shape this work to lean in their favor.

Historically in Appalachia, there are two classifications of magical work: one was thought to be by the Lord's hand, while the devil did the other. In translation, healing and protection were good work, while justified acts of curses and hexes were equated to malevolent work. The mountain folk practitioner often understands both assignments and is always keen on answering the call to do what is needed. *Need help with a cold? Got it. Want to hex your neighbor that's harassing you? Got that, too.*

The cultural blending of this patchworked region, combined with ancestral traditions and spirit connections, has led to a diverse array of mountain practitioners. As society moved away from the religious constraints of witch hunts and trials, there was room for a redefined witchcraft to emerge. In its present definition, witchcraft has taken on the reformed identity of having an interpersonal connection with one's spirit, animism, the practice of divination and rites, and an emphasis on contracts and relationships with various spirits. Witchcraft has historically involved working with another spirit. Without engaging with spirits—whether of folk saints, ancestors, nature, or otherwise—the practice remains, in a sense, empty.

The practice of modern witchcraft challenges the westernized mindset of individualism. For those with Appalachian roots, this can be particularly poignant healing work, as it addresses the scars left by previous generations. Generations of abandonment, exploitation, and broken promises have taught us to receive a helping hand with hesitation. I've learned that by opening up and putting aside my response of suspicion, the importance of both a physical and spiritual community becomes apparent. Mountain witchcraft invites us to return to our roots, both in an ancestral and a humanitarian sense.

LOCAL TALES OF WITCHES

In Appalachian witch lore, there are reoccurring themes such as good versus evil, power and knowledge, community and outsiders, nature and the supernatural, and morality and justice. These stories recount neighbors accusing others of causing some kind of community disruption, spinning a tale of nonsense they witnessed with their own two eyes! They'd express misfortunes like the hexing of cows, guns not shooting straight, churns not making butter, or bewitched individuals and animals that act out of sorts. You know, the things that would really rattle someone. This ultimately contributed to the deepening stereotypes and tropes surrounding witches, leading to this perception of witchcraft in Appalachia.

The thing about Southerners is that we like to talk. It is the oldest tradition to share what we overheard at the grocery store or through a friend of a friend about someone's neighbor. Sometimes, these stories were fabricated for entertainment, while other times, they were the whole truth. It's not done maliciously, but more as a way to look out for one another. Regardless, gossip had its place in a tight-knit community. Nobody went around doing nothin' that wouldn't be found out about, one way or another. As gossip spread, stories about unfamiliar neighbors began to blossom, and soon enough, there were supposed witches around the neighborhood. Whether there was a level of truth behind these spoken tales or not, when it came down to it, it didn't really matter. It was always better to be safe than sorry.

Uncle Johnnie of Raleigh County, West Virginia

Everyone's got a story about a man named Uncle Johnnie. If not, they've probably heard something relatively close, referring to an uncle who isn't really the storyteller's uncle. The term "witch" wasn't necessarily used to describe him, though there was speculation that he had a deal with the devil and was capable of throwing curses. This tale was originally recorded by folklorist Patrick W. Gainer.

Uncle Johnnie was someone who was described as strange or "funny." Not like *Haha* funny, but more like, *Oh, what's Johnnie got up his sleeve now?* In one story, he asked a local woman if he could use one of her two butter churns. She declined, saying she was using both churns every day with the amount of milk her cow produced. He sighed and said to her, "Alright, you can drink your milk, but I'll eat your butter."

That evening, after using the last of her butter and sharing it with neighbors, she tended her churn like usual. Except this time, the milk wouldn't churn. Well, that was odd indeed for her. Not long after that, her cows began to produce bloody milk. And that about was enough evidence that the woman needed to claim that Uncle Johnnie had put a hex on her.

She sent her husband after a local healer by the name of Uncle Jimmie Webb who knew of curing bewitchment. He visited her cows, whispering words under his breath that nobody could hear and left her with instructions to whip the evil out of her butter churns with a broom.

Meanwhile, local men not far away were hauling logs with Uncle Johnnie. He was giving them a helping hand until they recalled that suddenly, Uncle Johnnie began to scream and cry in complete agony. So much so, that they had to remove him from the work and find him a doctor.

This story, one we see time and time again, is an example of an accused perpetrator who bewitched someone's cattle. To treat the hex away, a witch doctor was sought after for instructions to cure their cattle. In this case, Uncle Jimmy Webb was known for having cures by whispering charms and "whipping" the cursed churns. A typical case of "good versus evil." Uncle Jimmy and Uncle Johnnie both shared the ability to do the work but did so for different reasons. While Johnnie could have been accused of witchery by causing harm to the cattle, Jimmy would never have been because his role was a helping hand rather than a nuisance.

Grandma of Booger Hole in Clay County, West Virginia

Another curious tale that rings familiar, recorded originally in Patrick W. Gainer's fieldwork, refers to a local woman's peculiar death. The story goes that an older woman who lived in Booger Hole was capable of bewitching others. She typically kept to herself and didn't have anyone else living with her at the house. One day, a young gentleman asked to use her mule for some farmwork. She agreed, laying out her rules. He was to take good care of her animal, and he made the promise that he would. After several days of hard labor, the young man returned her mule exhausted and famished. Out of anger, she cursed at the young man. For days, he roamed around town, talking to himself and acting completely out of character. He assumed he had been cursed into the madness by the woman. The young man was so unwell that he sought revenge and murdered her one night in hopes his madness would dissipate.

The Roan Mountain Witch, Carter County, Tennessee

I am very familiar with the tale of the Roan Mountain witch, as Roan Mountain was a frequent stop during late summer and early fall days. It's located on the border between North Carolina and Tennessee. The Roan Mountain witch didn't go by a particular name because nobody knew much about her. In fact, apparently it was best not to speak about her. Any mention of the witch's presence on the hilltop would evoke her spirit and unleash a hex causing emotional turmoil or other inconveniences.

When I was told the story, we were on this trail, and I remember envisioning the figure weeping into her hands while roaming around the bald.

For what? Nobody knew. Hikers and campers had reported hearing cries off in the distance at nightfall with no evidence of anyone camping nearby. It's an odd thing, really, and who knows if this witch was even real. The only recorded evidence other than what was told by locals is an article from 1901 in the *Louisville-Carter Journal*:

UP-TO-DATE STORIES OF WITCHCRAFT
With the North Carolina Mountains For a Background.
A Witch-Ridden District,
Where Aged Hags Hold The People In Subjection

As local gossip spread about rumored witches, every mishap seemed to be done by invisible hands. It was no longer just a coincidence. A stream of unfortunate events was chalked up to be the possible work of someone else. The line between coincidental and intentional blurred until accidents held a glimmer of malicious suspicion. In my household, we would speculate if odd things occurred in threes. If you stubbed your toe, then maybe it was bad timing. If you stubbed your toe and then broke a dish, then maybe keep an eye out. If you stubbed your toe, broke a dish, and then had a nightmare? Then we'd wonder if it was the act of someone, or something, else.

Eventually, the paranoia escalated into the idea that every eerie noise from the woods or an unfamiliar figure in the dark was proof that someone was dancing with the devil. Locals applied these preconceived notions to their suspicious neighbors and even to their own backwoods. There were stories of a shadowed figure rumored to live close by. In a nearby corner, the devil himself was lurking, ready to make a bargain with his next victim.

THE APPALACHIAN DEVIL

It is important that we establish the difference between *the devil* and *the Devil* with a capital "D." The Devil, known by other names like Satan, refers to a figure from Abrahamic religions. The Devil was known to be the counterpart of the Christian God. We're not discussing this specific figure in this context. Instead, we're exploring a more complex, regional-specific devil.

The Appalachian devil is a multifaceted being that is entangled in present-day folk songs and tales. In a place that embodies the unknown of nature and its mysteries, it is the perfect environment for such stories to grow such an entity. Each ancestor from across the pond and those who are native here already had their preconceptions of various devil-like figures. The Cherokee have stories pertaining to devil-like figures having the ability to cause physical illness to an individual. In European lore, the devil holds a bargainer's identity in exchange for materials and magical gifts, as well as knowledge. In some cases, the devil doesn't do his own dirty work, but instead has help from local witches who signed his contract. It seems like no matter where you look, you can't help but find the devil's fingerprints here.

While the Appalachian folkloric devil developed from this Christian lens, he also had his own regional identity, influenced by diverse cultural folktales. Spirits are inherently beyond the confines of gender, but stories tend to assign gendered characteristics from an older, conventional mindset of society. In this context, the Appalachian devil is depicted as a man and referred to as "he" in various tales. The folkloric devil had no agenda to overtake the Lord and conquer the world. Instead, he is keen on the idea of trickery, bribery, and causing neighborhood havoc, rather than convincing the conversion of someone's faith. He also goes by names like the Shadow Man or Old Scratch. He is depicted as a shadowed, unfamiliar figure in the woods or a strange man wandering about aimlessly on the roadside. Those who engaged with him had a chance to enter into contracts for personal gain by signing his book or risk losing their valuables, depending on his test.

There are numerous Appalachian tales that depict the nature of the devil in these mountains. In the story "The Devil and the Jug," the devil was tricked and trapped inside a jug by an angry witch. She threw the jug out only for a local mountaineer to discover it on his travels. With the need for money after a harsh year of bad luck, he took the talking jug with the devil inside to the local fair. He found a clever way to get the devil to talk so he could charge locals to hear him. When the man returned home with the earned money, he left the jug attended by his wife. The devil then made a deal with the woman that he'd grant her all the money and more if she were to uncork the jug. She did so, tempted by the relief of prosperity, and thus the devil was released. However, he went back on his word and took everything from the couple, including burning down their house.

Another tale associates the devil with a musical instrument: the fiddle. Thanks to an old friend of mine who shared the story with me, it's one I recall when thinking back on our times shootin' the shit. He'd make offhanded jokes about how he bartered with the devil, which is why he learned to play the fiddle in the first place. The story is quite popular with different variations that inspired the folk song "The Devil Went Down to Georgia."

The version I'm aware of is about two musicians who found themselves hiking up a mountain after hearing music play in the distance. Music, as we know, is a collective enjoyment, and local jam sessions are a way to get to know fellow neighbors. When they arrived at the scene, there was a party at a large house. They were invited inside and asked to take a seat and to play their quick-tempo tunes. Ever so delighted, the fiddlers began to play—and played hard they did. The stringed instruments were strumming at a quick pace together. Dancers were caught up in the euphoria and danced until their hearts couldn't stand it. Eventually, the devil himself arrived to join in on the town's fun.

While the party continued, the attendees noticed odd things about this strange man who arrived in high fashion, such as sharp eyes and goat-like feet. The crowd began to take notice of him more during such a jolly time, only to become stunned by his true appearance. But it was too late. He had danced with a woman 'til she fell over dead, and all the others fell on their knees too. When the clock struck midnight, the devil fled the scene and took the entire house with him. All that was left were the two fiddle players, who were so entranced from playing their music that they didn't even notice what was going on.

In fiddle lore, the devil had crafted the instrument himself to entice others to make barters with him by musical showdowns. Some of the popular folk ballads depict the devil as someone who enjoys games and riddles. "The Devil's Nine Questions" is an old song that demonstrates just that. This traditional ballad trickled over from the English and Scottish immigrants and had various versions recorded in the region. The story within the song involves the devil asking a series of riddles for the encountered individual to answer correctly. This version was recorded by Alan Lomax and sung by Gladden Texas and is available to listen to via the Library of Congress.

"The Devil's Nine Questions"

Oh, you must answer my questions nine,
Sing ninety-nine and ninety,
Or you're not God's, you're one of mine
And you are the weaver's bonny.

What is whiter than the milk?
Sing ninety-nine and ninety;
And what is softer than the silk?
And you are the weaver's bonny.
Snow is whiter than the milk,
Sing ninety-nine and ninety;
Down is softer than the silk,
And I am the weaver's bonny.

Oh, what is higher than a tree?
Sing ninety-nine and ninety;
And what is deeper than the sea?
And you are the weaver's bonny.
Heaven's higher than a tree,
Sing ninety-nine and ninety;
And hell is deeper than the sea,
And I am the weaver's bonny.

What is louder than a horn?
Sing ninety-nine and ninety;
And what is sharper than a thorn?
And you are the weaver's bonny.
Thunder's louder than a horn,
Sing ninety-nine and ninety;
And death is sharper than a thorn,
And I am the weaver's bonny.

What is more innocent than a lamb?

Sing ninety-nine and ninety;

And what is meaner than womankind?

And you are the weaver's bonny.

A babe is more innocent than a lamb,

Sing ninety-nine and ninety;

The devil is meaner than womankind,

And I am the weaver's bonny.

Oh, you have answered my questions nine,

Sing ninety-nine and ninety;

And you are God's, you're none of mine,

And you are the weaver's bonny.

In this traditional folk song, an individual can be released from the devil's grip by answering the riddles correctly. This reflects Appalachia's lore that although the devil may attempt to catch you in clever riddles, there are ways to protect oneself by outsmarting the spirit.

I often think about in what cases folks would find themselves in such a pickle to even toy with the idea of bartering with a figure they so fear. I can't help but conclude that in moments of such scarcity, any hand willing to help is worth it to save oneself and one's family. Like the tale of the man who took advantage of the devil in the jug and made a profit, all in the name of saving his family from a harsh winter with little to no food to survive. And yes, it may have ended up not paying off, which is why the lesson is often to avoid making deals with the devil, because it never plays out anyhow.

The Appalachian devil, much like witches, could shapeshift into animals. Old tales that spread from overseas mention that the devil is associated with black dogs. In England, there are stories of people selling their souls to the devil. After death, they'd reappear around graveyards and cemeteries as black hellhounds of the night. Another tale from London is the Black Dog of Newgate. An old scholar was taken as a prisoner on account of witchery. During the famine of this time, prisoners ended up killing the scholar to consume him. Those who were responsible for the man's death reported seeing a sinister black dog monitoring the prison. The black dog slowly killed each of the scholar's murderers until the last one fled the prison, only to be hunted down by the dog anyway.

The depiction of a black dog being associated with encountering the devil made its way into the Appalachian region, with similar folktales spreading through its roots. The Black Dog of the Blue Ridge from Botetourt County, Virginia, is one for comparison. The following telling is from Luke Bauserman:

> In the year 1683 the report was spread that at the wildest part of the trail in this pass there appeared at sunset a great black dog, who, with majestic tread, walked in a listening attitude about two hundred feet and then turned and walked back. Thus he passed back and forth like a sentinel on guard, always appearing at sunset to keep his nightly vigil and disappearing again at dawn. And so the whispering went with bated breath from one to another, until it had traveled from one end of the state to the other.
>
> Parties of young cavaliers were made up to watch for the black dog. Many saw him. Some believed him to be a veritable dog sent by some master to watch; others believed him to be a witch dog.

The story ends with the conclusion that the black dog was nothing other than a faithful ghostly companion to his owner, a lost traveler who died in the mountains, whose wife discovered his body seven years later.

She had traced her lost husband to Botetourt County and heard the story of the witch dog that paced the pathway every sunset. After convincing locals to take her to this place, she was led by the haunted dog to a boulder where her husband's and his canine's remains were buried. Thus, the dog did its duty to return his wife to him and was never seen again. However, the unfamiliar black dog's identity in local lore was closely tied to its reputation of witchcraft and its association with the devil.

While the Appalachian devil may be more inclined to entertain himself by tricking locals, the overall tone of speaking about the devil was still done in whispers. By speaking too loudly of his name, he may just show up at your doorstep with cunning intent. He knows how to uncover your deepest desires, offering a tempting bargain to fulfill them. For this reason, rumors spread that you wouldn't want him to know the whereabouts of your valuables as he might tempt you to haggle them away.

I've come to know this entity in a different light, as someone met at the crossroads. In between the pages written of this figure, the devil is a key holder to embracing the path of witchery. By venerating this spirit, the practitioner's work explores a path leading to personal autonomy and exploring deep desires. In a world that urges us to suppress who we truly are and live within certain societal structures, maybe the devil's quest is worth facing. After all, stories reveal that he unveils the truth we're afraid to admit, inviting a personal reckoning. While it's wise to keep your distance from strangers on your travels and steer clear of any fiddlin' or riddlin' to avoid losing valuables, there's another door worth opening.

APPALACHIAN INITIATION RITES

The initiation of walking the witch's path is a rite conducted with reverence and solemnity. In the southern region, the rite was performed to make a deal with the devil in exchange for profound magical knowledge and abilities. It was a way of claiming religious freedom in a rather historically conservative region. A chance to break free from societal confinements and embrace authenticity. This includes embracing older animistic beliefs aside from the deep-rooted Christian faith. It brought a sense of liberation from the religious boundaries of man-made rules and societal pressures by petitioning a spirit who represents such liberation. Walking this path meant embodying another side of the self—the one that has been described as "wild." To those who do not understand this path, the term *wild* refers to something that was assumed to be "unnatural"—but it's anything but. What can be unnatural about communing with the spirits here, there, and in between?

The devil serves as a regional folkloric representation of a guide in a witchcraft practice. In Appalachian lore, the focus is primarily to avoid his deception and trickery. A closer look reveals that he merely unveils the true desires of the people, offering them alternative paths that lead to their deepest longings and finding their unique place. For the mountain practitioner, making a pact with the devil is not done by manipulation. Instead, they knock on the door with consent in pursuit of liberation, magical abilities, and power. This "power" refers to reclaiming autonomy from their oppressors rather than dominating others. Instead, they'd use this power for seeking justice when rebalancing the scales was needed. To "call on the devil" is to request guidance in the witch's work. In this contract, practitioners recovered agency over their lives, breaking free from the restrictions imposed by society or circumstance. In a sense, the devil became not only a figure of temptation but also a catalyst for personal transformation and liberty.

The Appalachian rites take place in a liminal setting, such as mountaintops. The individual would hike up to the tallest spot nearby with the intention of renouncing their Christian faith in order to make a pact with the devil. In some rites, the individual is said to place one hand on the top of their head and the other at the bottom of their foot, similar to the historical recordings of other rites. In this intertwined position, they'd state a variation of an incantation thrice, such as, "Devil, take me, ring and all." Other rites included arriving before sunrise with a gun. While renouncing their Christian faith, they'd shoot the gun toward the rising Sun six times. With that, the devil would appear with his black book for the individual to sign in their own blood. In one recording from Knott County, Kentucky, a woman became a witch with a gun and a handkerchief on top of a hill. As the Sun began to rise, she lifted the handkerchief toward the Sun and shot one bullet through it while praying to the devil. The devil only accepted her request if the handkerchief bled.

While a gun and a bullet are repeatedly used in initiation rites, they are also used to rid a witch. Those who claimed to be cursed or hexed by a witch were the only ones who could accurately describe the apparent witch's identification. They'd give a description to the witch doctor to gain a better understanding of who their target should be. After they knew who the accused witch was, they would take a photo of them, pin it to a tree, and then shoot it with a silver bullet. This would physically manifest in defeating the witch's curse by removing whatever disturbance the victim was experiencing. In some cases, it would wound the suspected witch, too.

After making their deal with the devil, witches became capable of shapeshifting into animals. Countless stories of witch rabbits, dogs, cats, deer, and even raccoons are recalled along the vast region. One murderous tale tells of how locals were skeptical of an old woman and her suspicious bewitching tendencies. When a mysterious murder occurred, the community was quick to point the finger in the woman's direction. Several hunting men gathered to seek her out. As they dispersed on their quest, one returned, reporting that he saw a rabbit the same color as the woman's hair. Assuming she had taken the form of this rabbit, they began to direct their attention to hunt down the animal. On their hunt, one man found the rabbit, and shot a silver bullet at its leg. The wounded rabbit disappeared into the night. The following day, the old woman was found limping on the same wounded rabbit leg.

The devil and the Lord have equally had their presence here, each playing a role in the practitioner's work in the ongoing struggle between virtue and vice. We've come to understand that they can coexist. Now, don't get me wrong, I'm not suggesting that you need to make a pact with the devil if that's not your thing. I'm simply offering a different perspective on a figure who is often misunderstood in our stories. The classic narrative of good versus evil found its way into our mountains as a response to oppressive forces that sought to control and divide. But we've learned to offer prayers for our neighbors while also rebelling against those who abuse their power. In hindsight, the heinous acts blamed on the common people by their oppressors were not the work of the devil at all. They were instead acts done in the spirit of defending our vulnerable neighbors and ourselves, regardless of whom they upset.

4

TO HELP OR TO HARM: SOUTHERN MOUNTAIN FOLK PRACTITIONERS

We should clarify how folk magic may differ from witchcraft here, as these are key influences that inspire the work of modern folk practitioners. When I say "practitioners," I am referring to individuals who engage in magical practices, whether they practice folk magic, witchcraft, otherwise, or both. Folk magic is the result of regional and cultural beliefs related to superstitions, customs, and religion. Historically speaking, witchcraft includes spirit work with figures such as the devil, deities, and others while also engaging with the metaphysical.

Folk magic has a strange reputation of being viewed as a "lesser" magical practice compared to other approaches within the occult sphere. I'd have to disagree with this notion. The power of the people is strong. Think of how much change can occur when a group of people unite. The notion of utilizing what is readily available at our fingertips is also powerful. There are no limitations—only opportunities. It is often woven into the practitioner's daily life of perceiving unlimited methods by using what is already available. It's accessible with no requirement of fancy tools or complex rituals.

Today, practitioners of both folk magic and witchcraft may identify as *folk witches*, despite the region's historical avoidance of the term. This term has begun circulating to provide context to the outsider that the practitioner interweaves these two approaches together, resulting in an ancestral and personal magical practice that incorporates their culture, traditions, healing practices, spirit contracts, the land, rituals and workings, and energy work. While it may seem contradictory to outsiders, this practice emphasizes personal efficacy, rather than a strict adherence to a specific doctrine.

The early mountain practitioners from all backgrounds and genders had a profound respect for the wisdom woven into southern Appalachia. While some acquired their practice directly from Mamaw or Papaw, or were born with spiritual gifts, others resurrected traditional customs through the guidance of publications, spirit relationships, and their connection to the land.

For those reviving folk practices, it can feel like finding a way back home to themselves by embracing ancestral knowledge. Each practitioner will have their approach to doing things directed by their personal gnosis and any mentorship. For example, a practitioner from up north in the region may have a different approach to a healing charm from down south. The region is vast, with many hands involved. I have met practitioners from the same county whose work varies from my own. It makes it challenging to conclude that Appalachian folk magic has a singular playbook. Our unique family stories and experiences have a direct influence on how we do this work.

However, there will be synchronization because of the shared culture and land. We may all recognize the potency of specific plants here, like goldenrod. Goldenrod sings about the end of summer and the welcoming of fall. Inspired by Cherokee medicine, we may brew goldenrod in our teas to help with inflammation or grind its flowers for a healing salve. The same goes for reciting verses from the Book of Psalms. Utilizing the Bible was traditionally practiced, especially for those who were required to convert their ancestral traditions into the Christian framework. The list of similarities continues between the traditions that are uniquely part of Appalachia's fabric as they cross-pollinated with one another and adapted with time. Their family story, personal gnosis, and environment will all have a delicate hand in cultivating the practitioner's work.

Those skilled in magical practices shared their knowledge among those in their close-knit communities. Yet some households closed their doors to keep important matters private when executing their work. Privacy is power. Practitioners kept their work close to their chest to prevent others from knowing how to counter their magic. Securing a familial practice was a well-kept secret. In times of community need, though, they'd step out from the shadows to offer their hand. Other times, it was best to be more reserved. In small towns, one whisper is all it takes before everyone knows of someone or something that could be weaponized against another. In the tight confines of rural life, one tiny rumor could ignite a wildfire of gossip, leaving practitioners vulnerable regardless of their well intentions.

Sympathetic magic is a foundational concept within folk magic frameworks. It is the belief that actions on one object can influence a corresponding target in the physical realm that it is intended to represent. Sympathetic magic may be an old approach, but it is not forgotten and is still very effective.

This type of magic is underpinned by two principles. The first is the *law of similarity*, where an object resembling a subject can be directly affected. Take, for example, a doll made from cloth or rags crafted to represent a targeted person. Whatever is then done to the doll will manipulate the influence

on the recipient. The second principle is the *law of contagion*, which suggests that any personal belonging of an individual is tethered to their energy. This enables successful workings using items like hair or fingernail clippings to exert magical influence. Once something has been in contact with the person, whether hair or their footprint, it is bound to them.

Fruits and vegetables would be used as a device to present the target in mind. Pins can be immersed into the fruit to bind and stall their subject. In some cases, a designated tree would do the job, too. Recorded from western Virginia within the Pennsylvania Dutch practice, whenever there was friction among neighbors, the practitioner would visit a neighboring fruit tree and "put a pin in it." But this wasn't always for revenge. The method of using a tree is also done to help heal an individual. To cure sickness, a person's clothes could be soaked in the nearby river and then tied to a tree. An old Scots-Irish healing method would have parents pass their sickly children over a tree stump to transfer the illness.

Practitioners with profound abilities of healing and taking care of spiritual matters were known by a multitude of names depending on their specific skill set, reputation, and location. If the practitioner was on good terms with local folk, then they'd be referred to by others for their services, whereas if they were suspected of being up to no good, then their reputation would be tainted and they would be avoided. It wasn't uncommon for someone to have a complex reputation. Both things can be true, and folk practitioners and witches stand in the betwixt of this truth.

MOUNTAIN FOLK PRACTITIONERS

Perhaps a local woman was known as the granny witch for helping women deliver children and herbal remedies during postpartum. Meanwhile, she may also hold the gift of second sight, or Sight, and dabble in people's love lives. She would play several roles in the community—a midwife by day, a conjurer by night. Some may seek her guidance, while others may avoid her out of fear she'd curse their relationships. Many of the folk practitioner labels and jobs crossed over into one another: a witch, a doctor, a conjurer, a healer. The practitioner will sometimes wear multiple hats. The following is a short list of familiar descriptions of magical workers along this region, but let it be known that this is not the only list, as some practitioners may have other ways to describe themselves and their work.

Witch Doctors

The practitioners sought after for their counter work against witchcraft were known as witch doctors, faith healers, or power doctors. These doctors were capable of locating bewitchment and, in some cases, the accused witch.

Among the most notorious afflictions is the cursing of livestock. Under this suspicion, the cow would no longer be "giving down" the milk. Instead, it would be producing bloody milk. The witch doctor would be called to cure the afflicted cattle. As a cure, they would take the cursed milk, dig a hole, and either beat it with a thorned stick or burn a *ticket* (the Pennsylvania Dutch term for a written prayer or petition) and cast it into the tainted bloody milk to set fire with kerosene.

Other doctors would counter bewitchment by marking up an image of the suspect of witchery and hang it on a tree. They'd craft a witch's ball made up of cow or horsehair to be used as a bullet, then throw the witch's ball at the image. Wherever the ball hit, a physical wound would manifest on the suspect. The witch doctor was someone with a positive reputation in the community. They were known to be "good witches" because they practiced in the Lord's name, often referencing the Bible in their work, and were capable of countering the work of another.

Southern Conjurers

Here in the South, the term *conjurer* became synonymous with a practitioner who works within the framework of African spiritual practices and traditions. A conjurer's work can sometimes include invoking a variety of spirits such as folk saints, angels, ancestors, and the Lord. As a result, the Southern conjurer takes on the role of both a spirit worker and faith healer, merging magical traditions with mountain faith to provide remedies, protection, and spiritual guidance. Some conjurers are also known to have the gift of Sight and utilize divination methods to help address their clients' needs.

The conjurer may also embody the dual role of a rootworker. The rootworker is a practitioner that specializes in the folk healing within Hoodoo tradition, which emerged from the blending of the African diaspora and Indigenous herbalism in the Southern states. To carry the title of rootworker often meant implementing the materia medica in healing remedies, rituals, and magical work.

Particularly in the Southern hills and low country regions, the conjurer or rootworker became a central figure to those seeking justice and relief from ailment. They provided remedies for physical and spiritual needs, offered guidance in situations, empowered their clients against oppression and injustice, and also assisted in personal matters such as finances, relationships, and seeking lost items.

Grannies or Appalachian Witches

Before the regulation of modern medicine, grannies, or Appalachian witches, were sought after for their herbal remedies influenced by European and Indigenous traditions. Grannies were known to focus primarily on women's health. They obtained knowledge from their mothers about natural medicine and folk methods when modern medical resources were limited. Their healing methods included but were not limited to herbal medicine. This herbal knowledge was also learned by exchange with Cherokee, Creek, and other tribes.

While grannies stood in positions between life and death, they were also in tune with the spiritual and physical realms. Their intuition was heightened by their experience working within this liminal space. Sometimes, they were born with abilities such as Sight, which provided spiritual guidance in addition to herbal medicine.

These matriarchs, often called on for their midwifery, not only tended the birth of local children but also were well-known for matters of the hearth and home. They tended to domestic responsibilities, ensuring their home was a safe space. They cared for their children and their community by answering house calls. They're not to be taken advantage of, though. Like the mother bear, anything that is a potential threat would result in immediate protection. They knew how to counter magic, assess situations with divination, and keep local gossip. This is one of the ways that word got around town. Gossip, despite some negative connotations, has revived many of our local folktales. Due to the patriarchal society, midwives and grannies were not immune to false accusations of witchery. They restricted their work to the safety of their own home or between trusted neighbors.

Yarb Doctors

Yarb was a term that meant "herb" in the Southern region. Yarb doctors were known for their cunning ways and extensive herbal knowledge. Their work didn't always involve invoking a spirit or incorporating magical frameworks. The focus was more on natural medicine, similar to the granny, rootworker, and other herbalists. The yarb doctor's work was entangled in roots beneath the soil. Their apothecary cabinets were filled with generations of knowledge passed down to them by Europeans, Africans, and Indigenous communities, a culmination of the region's rich herbal medicine. Their natural solutions helped heal the body. A yarb doctor would gain recognition for their tried-and-true methods.

Yarb doctors were of the mountain faith, and prayers were sometimes incorporated while preparing a medicinal solution such as a salve, poultice, tincture, or tea. Yarb doctors had an intimate relationship with the land, bearing knowledge of the mountain landscape and its rich native flora.

Burn Whisperers, Blood Stoppers, Wart Doctors

There are some mountain practitioners and healers whose work is very specific. The healers' titles are self-explanatory: Burn whisperer. Blood stopper. Wart doctor. Blood stoppers could stop blood in wounds. Burn whisperers could whisper burns out of the skin. Wart doctors were known to cure warts by speaking directly to them.

Blood stoppers and burn whisperers were born with the Gift, often said to be the seventh son or daughter of the seventh son or daughter. This belief was brought over from the Scots-Irish immigrants. Burn whisperers, blood stoppers, and wart doctors obtained the prayers for this work through someone who also practiced of the opposite sex. These healers had positive reputations when cures couldn't be handled otherwise. In Southern families, someone always knew someone who had the Gift. For some, it was their own family member, and in that case, you were always in good hands.

Water Witches

Water witches were known for their ability to locate water sources, which was a very helpful skill to have. Dowsing is a specific form of divination that locates water underground, along with other objects such as metals, oils, and the like. A specific tool called a dowsing rod is used. The dowsing rod can be made by a fallen tree branch that is forked in the shape of a Y.

In this practice, the practitioner would hold the dowsing rod by the two ends underhanded, exposing their palms to the sky with the rod pointing outward in a horizontal form. The water dowser would enter a trance, allowing the end of the rod to guide them toward the water source underground. Their grip is slightly loose, not to control the dowsing rod themselves, but instead to intuitively follow its pull.

When approaching a water source, the dowsing rod would bend toward the ground to locate it. There are a number of local stories that confirm this divination technique, despite some local skepticism. Today, some practitioners still use this divination method and can locate wells or oil before digging, and even lost items.

MUNDANE ITEMS FOR MAGIC

Household superstitions may have been viewed with skepticism, but what lies beneath them is knowledge often disregarded. While mountain super-stitions may highlight an era of paranoia, they are an opportunity for the attentive practitioner to take a closer look at the magic that may lie beneath the layers. The most familiar mountain magic uses plant matter, but other aspects of it require recognizing items around the comfort of your home.

Plant spirits are an important element, absolutely. But so is the broom in your closet, the paper found in your journal, and the power behind your spoken words.

Being resourceful goes a long way. In a region that relied heavily on this skill set, it makes sense that it's reflected in its folk magic. My dad always encouraged me to think outside the box. A man known for his creative and outlandish inventions. I suspect he adopted this mindset from generations before him, which was then instilled in me. This led me to reconsider any pressure to buy fancy tools for an effective working.

You'll notice that I use both *spell* and *working* throughout this book. Sometimes, I even combine the two. But let's not get tied up in its semantics. I tend to use them interchangeably out of pure habit. Personally, I feel like using the term *working* is the best way to explain to an outsider the reality of a spell. I think it provides a better interpretation of what it entails. It is a craft. Something that is meant to be practiced, to experiment with and adapt according to results. Done with our attentive minds and hands. An energy work of transmutation and influence, a collaboration between me and spirits, and that requires my undivided attention.

Though an exhaustive list of items that have the potential for magical workings would be quite lengthy, there are some commonly used items that are easily accessible. There's room for customization and to think outside the box. Specific traditional methods that the healer, conjurer, or witch follows in their practice can also inspire how a mundane tool is used magically. The purpose behind the work at hand is considered. Are we protecting someone? Are we protecting ourselves? Are we turning the table so someone gets what they deserve? Are we attracting or removing something? You get the point. Many of these tools have dual purposes—both for healing and malice. How they can be employed is up to you, your spirits, and your work.

Beans

When it comes to the topic of using beans, I immediately consider the famous story of "Jack and the Beanstalk." If you're not familiar with the story, Jack sold the family's only cow for a pack of magical beans that would grow high into the clouds, where he would climb to meet a giant. During Jack's sneaky visits, he stole coins from the giant that he would give to his mother. This tale positions the magical beans as the tether to Jack's wealth building (though I do not condone the fact that he *stole* the giant's coins).

Consuming black-eyed beans on New Year's Eve is a Southern custom originating from the Civil War era and is part of the African American tradition of Hoodoo. The black-eyed bean crops withstood the war era, becoming a key source of nutrients for families. This dish, with its many variations, entered the mountain region and became a tradition for Black and white households. Black-eyed beans symbolize resilience for the freed African Americans and represent wealth and good fortune. The traditional dish is prepared with collard greens, representing money, and cornbread, representing gold, to attract an abundant year.

Beans can be employed in workings to help grow something or to decay something by the act of counting. Take a set number of black-eyed beans and pray over one while placing it into a jar. One at a time on each day. Begin this on a New Moon and continue until the Full Moon to help grow an area of your life, like finances. If you'd like to diminish something, like stopping someone from speaking ill about you, begin at the first Waning Moon phase and complete on the New Moon. Beans can also be used as filler in homemade fabric charms to attract prosperity and abundance. The charm can be stored around the home or worn by the practitioner.

Bottles

Decoy bottles are employed to help counteract the working of another. Archaeologists in the Appalachian region have recovered some of these bottled charms. A glass medicine vial retrieved from  Armstrong Farmstead in Fayette County, Kentucky, was reportedly from sometime between 1810 and 1850. Its containments inlcuded four straight pins in unfamiliar liquid. In 1915, a bottle was restored from Watauga County, North Carolina, with containments unknown that had been sealed and strung in a loft, assumed to "scare the witches out of the house."

These historical artifacts are physical evidence of older ways making their way over, feeding into the superstitions that witches and other unwanted spirits could be trapped in these bottles. The containments of such decoys included urine or other personal belongings to protect the targeted individual. The bottle would also include items that would destroy the bewitchment. Nails or pins were utilized to nail down the witch's work. They would be tightly secured before storing in the thresholds or crevices of the home.

While some bottles were discreetly positioned, others were displayed as obvious wards against evil. The African tradition of bottle trees, featuring cobalt blue bottles positioned all over various branches, was intended to combat evil spirits. I recall driving down a back road with a friend and recognizing this ward placed in someone's front yard. What may look like an interesting sculpture is actually an imitation of the African folk art from Congo. The color blue symbolizes water because it is believed that evil spirits cannot cross water. This specific color is also referred to as haint blue. The word *haint* comes from the Gullah folklore prevalent in the Deep

South. It refers to a haunting or spirit. I've seen this ward applied even in the southern mountains and over in northern counties of South Carolina. Some folks don't restrict themselves to just the cobalt blue bottles for their protective trees; various colored bottles could be used to distract evil spirits away from the home.

Additional shiny objects such as pots and tin cans were used to distract unwanted spirits, witches, and even faeries. My mother once displayed old, various multicolored jars and bottles above her windowsill. I couldn't help but assume that this was an act to deflect negative energy, whether she was fully aware of it or not.

Broom

Keeping the house tidy and free of unwanted dirt or energy is crucial for maintaining spiritual hygiene. This ensures that nothing is lingering around that shouldn't be. When we cross the threshold of our front doors, we can bring in all sorts of energy collected throughout the day. Sweeping the house was timed after sunrise and before sundown to keep the family's good luck inside. Otherwise, it would be swept out of the home and pose a threat of bad luck to the household.

To eliminate any unwanted energies inside the home, you can begin sweeping from the back of the house toward the front. Sweep the collected dust away from your property, like at the end of your driveway, or discard it at a nearby crossroads. Sweeping could also remove someone from your life simply by sweeping under their feet or bed while they're sleeping. A broom is a tool that can be used to sweep curses or hexes away from the afflicted person.

I've always started from the top of the head and worked my way down to remove any evil eye or ill intention.

European stories associate witches with their broom, which was used to transport them inside their enemies' homes or to meet with other spirits like the devil. For this reason, the broom has also been used to stop a witch in their tracks. For preventative measures, a broom would be left outside the front door because it's said that witches could not step over it.

Candles

Candles are a very accessible tool that can either be purchased or homemade. Candles have become conduits for spirit communication. They are a light source to draw the attention of and serve as offerings to spirits, saints, angels, ancestors, deities, or otherwise. They represent the element of fire and can be used to harness energy for workings and prayers.

They have long been used in various traditions and folk magic, with many different styles to choose from, including customized molded candles. Before mass production, handmade dipped taper candles served as a primary light source and a ritual tool. They were originally made from tallow or animal fat, and eventually beeswax, which provided a cleaner burn. Personally, I enjoy making my own taper candles out of local beeswax. Specific corresponding herbs, colors, and even customized shapes can be considered in candle magic that pertains to the intended work. The number of candles used in a working can also be considered, like using the number of candles specific to the number of people involved.

Vigil candles, also known as seven-day candles, are often used for workings that require a longer duration. These candles are encased in glass and can be carefully dressed with oils and herbs aligned with the intent. They are commonly used for petition work and calling upon a specific spirit for assistance.

While writing this book, I crafted a petition candle for Mercury, the planetary energy associated with communication and writing. Each evening, I sat down to prepare for my writing session; I'd anoint the candle with a specific infused oil and recite my prayer written on a piece of paper that was taped around the glass. While the candle burned, the energy of Mercury extended their offer throughout the writing and editing process. Is it a coincidence that I began editing my manuscript during the first day of Mercury in retrograde? I don't believe so!

Coins

Coins don't just come in handy at the local gas station; they also hold significant value in protection matters. Silver is used to ward off malicious spirits and bewitchment, as we've observed in local witch lore. The British silver coin, sixpence, was used as a potent charm in the recordings of English and Scots-Irish immigrants. From the 17th to 19th centuries, the Celtic cross symbol was engraved in these coins. They were carried in one's pocket with the protective cross as a ward against witches.

The very name "sixpence" carries a sense of security, as it's a multiple of the number three—a number significantly used in folk practices as a reference to the Holy Trinity. This tradition of using coins in protective charms translated to the Southern region. Silver coins can be strategically placed around the house, stored in charm bags hung in windows, or carried as personal amulets. A friend once told me their local shop was experiencing some spiritual disturbances. They placed silver coins along the windowsills as an effective protective barrier.

Coins can also be used for money magic. We had a large jug in our household filled with spare coins growing up. In a way, it served as the household's money jar. At the end of the year, we'd go to the store coin dispenser to cash it out and would spend the proceeds on gifts for the holiday season.

During my first visit to my partner's hometown in England, I was gifted a 50p with Peter the Rabbit on it. Rabbits have become an important animal in my practice. Many folktales relate to them being associated with the Moon and traveling in between realms. For this reason, I use this silver coin for divination purposes for inquiries that are either yes or no. It's been helpful for decision-making, like moving forward with an intended spell working.

Iron

Far and wide, many believed that iron held protective energy. The region still employs iron in charms to protect oneself and one's kin. Iron nails were discovered in decoy bottles from long ago. These bottles contained a number of ingredients, but they consistently had iron nails as a means to hold down energy. Additionally, iron from a cast-iron cooking pan is used in protection magic—it creates a barrier to avoid any external energy interference. Meals prepared in a cast-iron dish can also hold the protective energy. To further iron's potency, the story of Jesus being nailed to the cross with three irons nails also informed practitioners of its significance. Various folk recordings described nails being driven into the thresholds of homes as a way to prevent the entrance of an unwanted individual or spirit.

Iron horseshoes were easy to access and put to use for home protection. They can be found positioned outside barn doors and above front doors. I've hung a horseshoe above doorways facing up secured with nails for protection of my residence, which is a common protective and good luck charm. You'll come across the debate of whether a horseshoe should be mounted facing up or down, but I've been taught facing up so the good luck and protection doesn't spill out. However, if you've been taught for it be facing down so that you're blessed when you cross the threshold, that's just as valid.

Jewelry

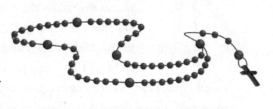

When considering enchanted jewelry for folk magic, the rosary comes to the forefront of my mind. In Catholicism, the rosary is not necessarily used as an accessory but more so as a statement of faith when worn with respect. It is held in the hands of the individual while reciting a prayer, using the beads as a guide in their spoken words.

This same concept can be applied when crafting a custom piece of jewelry made of material like beads. Specific colors and the number of beads can all be considerations in how the practitioner designs it. Other charms with symbols may be included for further customization. I myself have dedicated prayer beads used to connect with my familial spirits. They contain charms like a lighthouse to represent guidance during troubling times of emotional waves. Crafting a piece of jewelry can also be a devoted act to a particular spirit.

In the same vein, should you obtain an ancestral piece of jewelry, it can also be used to connect with their spirits. It can be worn for workings where you want to invoke the ancestor's spirit and call for their guidance. Enchanted jewelry that is handcrafted can also be made for protection. The act of jewelry-making is an example of magical work, with energy infused in each bead strung together and symbolic charm added, and finished with tying the final knot to complete the work.

Keys

Keys can help us unlock new doors of opportunity, enter through spiritual doorways, or secure our safety by locking a door. I say "door," but I'm referring to liminal spaces that allow the passage of spirits. A skeleton key is a key that can unlock all doors. Skeleton keys were popular in the Middle Ages and were given to the working class of castles and upper-class households. They were also called "pass keys," as they could pass anywhere without going through a main entrance. Crafted out of iron or brass, the key was not only capable of unlocking physical doors but also employed to unlock liminal doorways.

Keys can help unlock doors or pathways that would otherwise leave the practitioner feeling stagnant. They can also keep things secret and secure, away from prying eyes or lingering ears. They can also be used as a protection charm from unwanted visitors and spirits. Anoint a key with oil while reciting Psalm 91:14 for protection against spiritual attack or unwanted energies cast by others, then store the key at the home's thresholds. You may use this alternative prayer: "Under the protection of my wise and well ancestors, I am shielded in a love that will sustain me."

Mirrors

It is said that mirrors have the ability to keep a deceased loved one within the home if the mirror is not adequately covered after the person's death. This connection with the spiritual realm implies that the mirror is a doorway. For this reason, mirrors are great for divination or insight into hidden matters or targeted subjects. Place a lit candle in front of a mirror without any other lighting. Spend a few moments inquiring what you would like to see. Gaze into the mirror's reflection with the candlelight and record any visuals for interpretation.

Mirrors are also used for protective work. When sending something back to someone, like a nasty attitude or injustice, you can use the mirror to reflect their work back to them. If a mirror isn't handy, consider using other reflective surfaces such as tin foil.

Mirrors can also be used for personal reflective work. I find that having a mirror allows me to connect with my spirit. When reciting an incantation while looking in the mirror, witnessing myself saying these things helps in accepting them. Speaking kindly to yourself in the mirror is just one method for practicing self-love, and I've found it rather effective in my personal work.

Scissors

Scissors are used for protection and healing workings. They have the ability to sever unwanted connections, such as energetic ties, pain, troubles, or harmful influences. The act of cutting with the scissors' sharp edges represents cutting away any tethers that could create a blockage for an afflicted individual. Breaking free from situations or people that no longer serve you can be helpful in establishing and reinforcing boundaries in both the physical and spiritual realms. Scissors  have also been used to cut away pain by reinforcing the idea of removing something harmful from the body or spirit. We'll discuss more about how scissors have been traditionally applied in healing practices later on.

String/Cord/Yarn

 A personal favorite tool of mine that is accessible and yet very powerful is string, cord, yarn, or any kind of thread. You can get creative with the colors when it comes to your crafting. There are some color correspondences, such as red for protection and white for purification. I find inspiration in the seasons and the energy of my spirits to help me select the exact color scheme. With this threaded material, knot magic is performed by tying knots into the string/cord/yarn, with each knot imbued with the practitioner's intent with either spoken or thoughtful prayer.

The number of knots can play a significant role. You can tie a specific number of knots to count down to an important event, like a job interview, empowering each knot with the intention of success or confidence until the day arrives. A multiple of three is also a popular number in folk magic with its correspondence to the Holy Trinity, such as three, six, and nine. These numbers are traditionally considered in healing and protective workings.

A witch's ladder can also be made out of your chosen thread. Gather three strings of your choosing and weave them together, either by twisting them or braiding them. You can embellish the ladder with natural elements, such as flowers and twigs that correspond with the intent. The intentional ladder can be stored at the altar, as an offering, or at a designated place within the home, like above the door or hearth.

The various forms of threads are also useful for binding work. Binding candles or dolls represents restricting unwanted behaviors or neutralizing negative influences. The thread acts as a lock to put something into place, ensuring the work is contained and secured. Alternatively, natural thread can be bound to a healing tree to help transfer the trouble or sickness from the afflicted person to the tree.

FROM MAMAW'S BOOK OF SPELLS:
Take It to the Tree

Knot magic and cord magic go hand in hand. There are rituals that tie people together, like the ceremony of union between two people with a braided cord called handfasting. It even begins in the mother's womb, with a cord connecting her to the child for nourishment and growth. In this powerful impression of capturing the spirit of an intent, strings of all kinds can play a role as a physical representation.

The use of red cord or thread for protection can be traced back to a Bible story found in Genesis 38 where a midwife marked a first-born twin baby's wrist with a red cord. In the Pennsylvania Dutch practice, wool that was dyed red would be used for healing rites by passing the thread over the body of the sick, then hanging it on the hearth.

The magic of red thread weaves itself through various stories, deepening its correspondence of spiritual protection and ties to healing work for many practitioners. In this working, the intention is to take red thread and incorporate knot magic by imbuing the knots tied into the thread with the desire of emotional or physical healing.

To try it yourself, first decide what kind of red thread you'd like to use. There are many options available at local craft stores. I personally prefer to use environmentally friendly natural fibers. Dying your own red thread is also an option that only makes the working more personal. Some ingredients that result in red color tones are beets, hibiscus, and crab-apple bark.

Once you have your red thread prepared and on hand, dip it in blessed water and allow it to dry fully. Then measure the thread around your left wrist. The left hand ties us to our heart, and because this is a heart-center working, I find that this is most appropriate. As you begin to tie nine knots into the thread, recite this prayer inspired by Psalm 103: "I ask Spirit to take away sickness, infirmity, and emotional pain from me and restore me to good health."

Take the knotted red string to a local dogwood tree. Tie the string around one of the branches, and allow the tree to heal the distress. After seven days, return to the tree and untie the string. Cut it up into tiny pieces, burn it, and bury the ashes away from your property.

FROM MAMAW'S BOOK OF SPELLS:
Bury Their Words

The practice of dirt magic or working with soil collected from specific locations has roots in Southern folk practices. Graveyard dirt is used in foot-track magic specifically within the Hoodoo tradition. Soil from churches is used in Irish folk medicine practices for its healing properties. The soil was collected in a cloth and used to cover wounds. Mud collected from local rivers was also used to cure skin diseases. The shared belief that soil from a specific location held corresponding energies of healing or banishing explains why items might be dropped off or buried, as well as why soil might be gathered from a particular place for an intended magical working.

Now, let's get our hands a little dirty. Nobody is immune to sour words spoken of them. Whether it's to our face or behind our backs, salty words are bound to sting old wounds. If confronting the individual doesn't work, and taking matters into your own hands is better, this working can help bury the person's bitterness. It may appear simple, but it is effective.

On a piece of paper, write down what it is that the individual said. If you know their name, write that as well. Spit on the piece of paper—like you mean it, too! Roll the piece of paper away from you, binding it with thread. As you do so, recite the following: "Remove my name from your lip, may no other gossip sly or slip." Once the paper is sealed and bound, bury it in the soil of a thick hedge to create a barrier between you and the individual.

5

THE MOUNTAIN'S HELPING HANDS:
FOLK HEALING IN SOUTHERN APPALACHIA

I had a school friend who was very knowledgeable about natural medicine. I'm not entirely sure where she learned all that she knew. I never felt the need to ask. Anytime I suffered from a common cold or sore throat, or felt anxious, she'd offer a helping hand with a natural concoction she'd bring from her home. Mason jars in her room were filled with herbs of all sorts. Tiny little amber dropper bottles containing whatever she'd crafted that weekend filled the medicine cabinet.

She had become my own herbal healer and soul caretaker. Some days, she'd invite me over to brew tea together and consult about high school life. We'd not only enjoy a hot beverage during the colder months, but she also provided a safe space for counsel. She had a way of listening to you. Never once gave off the impression that you were intruding on her or anything like that. It was genuine. Her demeanor was soft and comforting, but stern like a lion to encourage boundary enforcement. At one point, we were really close before she graduated and moved to New Orleans. But not before she instilled some of her knowledge in me. She waved her pointer finger in my direction, looked me dead in the eyes, and urged me to take echinacea to help strengthen my immune system before winter fell, then gave me a tight squeeze.

Though I didn't obtain any herbal knowledge from a direct family member, friends like her and neighbors stepped in. They taught me that taking a spoonful of local honey would help seasonal allergies—but it had to be local, not just any kind from the grocery store. They taught me how to identify elderberry and make homemade cough syrup. They shared tea blends made with lemon balm, rose, and holy basil to help ease an aching heart.

There is something about discovering folk remedies that may appear so simple but make a great impact. I reflect on my ancestors, the ones I never got a chance to meet, and how they must have gone about curing and healing in times of sickness. I had heard about how my relatives, the ones who were coal miners, suffered at a young age from black lung. I had also heard of other familial illnesses and thought about how their relatives provided for them in those moments. Perhaps my paternal great-grandfather, a pastor, was also a faith healer. My mind wandered as I dove into my family stories. . . .

B efore medical doctors made their way into the rural mountains, people relied heavily on herbal remedies passed down by those who knew the work. This was either a family member or someone who knew someone not too far away. There was always someone nearby who could answer the call in times of crisis before medical physicians were readily available. As immigrants entered Appalachia, they found that some of their familiar herbal medicines were either unavailable or too costly to import. Out of necessity, they adapted to the new region using resources from their own backyard, inspired by the medicine of Indigenous People. The ability to maintain good health and cure illnesses relied on this exchange. The Indigenous People, with their relationship with the land and natural cures, are the original healers of this region. The plant knowledge of the Cherokee laid the groundwork for what became of southern Appalachian healing medicine. The enslaved African peoples found common ground in this medicine, blending their practices with Indigenous methods to craft remedies that were effective, accessible, and connected to the land.

Healers of the African diaspora were generally uninterested in incorporating European healing methods into their cures. As white physicians began to treat patients in enslaved communities, they consulted local Black healers when their medical remedies fell short. These physicians would observe the effectiveness of the herbal poultices and blends crafted by Black healers, who could heal the sick in a matter of days. Unfortunately, as the American South history tends to go, white physicians adopted these remedies into their medical handbooks. They claimed many of these healing remedies as their own, erasing the working hands of African healers and their wealth of knowledge from the region's medicinal landscape.

The undeniable cultural exchange began to take root in the southern mountains as social classes between races began to blur. Self-preservation and self-reliance became shared values in the hills, especially as working-class laborers faced some of the same health issues. Southern folk healing isn't a segregated practice as it was part of both white and Black households. It wasn't just faith that led these communities to share their healing ways, but it was also the shared value of being a good neighbor. As physicians struggled to reach the rugged mountain regions, the health-care system expanded slowly, leaving minimal access to medical aid. The mountaineers continued to rely heavily on their local healers.

Living side by side on the same mountains, these neighbors shaped each other's healing traditions in ways that can still be experienced today. While the European diaspora had their ways, it's impossible to fully understand the vast healing landscape without also recognizing the deep roots of the African diaspora healers and Indigenous herbal medicine knowledge. Their remedies left a lasting impression in the teas brewed, salves poured, and tinctures crafted. These traditions created a regional healing well. Deep and ever-flowing. A cure to ease the mind, body, and spirit.

THE SOUTHERN MOUNTAIN HEALER

Folk recordings of local healers reveal common pillars of this practice, combining both the physical and spiritual well-being of an individual. Healers will have their own remedies depending on their location, the materials that are available, and their ancestral background. Some healers obtained knowledge from a family member or fellow healer. Regardless, mountain healers were the region's helping hands long before modern medicine existed.

The local healer was the first person to call in a place where it took doctors, usually residing a few counties over, too long to arrive. Dangerous accidents caused by farming equipment could be fatal if not addressed quickly. And unfamiliar diseases were quick to take the lives of the young and elderly. The local healer had a sense of responsibility to put their good work to use. As I've stated, it's always better for me to paint the picture of such a situation through storytelling. Inspired by folk recordings, many of them went a little something like this:

A local girl had fallen ill with a high fever. Her mother's concern led her to call a kind woman who goes by the name Granny Sue. She was no stranger, and in fact was the same healer who tended to the woman after she had given birth.

Granny Sue didn't hesitate to accept the call. She packed her belongings, including a decoction of cherry-tree bark and a long thread of red yarn. She made haste to go down the road through the winding pathway. As soon as she arrived, she set down her belongings and sat beside the bedridden daughter, placing her hand on her forehead.

The mother informed Granny Sue of the young girl's demeanor leading up to falling sick, with the healer making mental notes of the most minor details. A delicate exchange happened between the healer and the sick. She tentatively listened, gathering as much mundane information as possible to determine the next step.

As the mother finished describing how the young girl had fallen ill during the winter months, Granny Sue placed a pot of water on the stovetop to begin brewing the cherry-bark tea. She described the remedy to the mother, showing her what the cherry bark looked like, and where to find some, and provided brewing instructions.

Granny Sue placed a damp cloth on the young girl's forehead. "There, there," she muttered. With the red yarn in hand, she sat beside the young girl and counted the number of times the girl coughed, tying a single knot every time. "One, two, three, four . . ." Four knots were tied into the yarn as she muttered words of a prayer too low for anyone to hear.

Once the tea was ready, she handed it to the mother with clear instructions that it must be consumed entirely for three consecutive days to help break the fever.

The healer bid farewell and left their home. On her way, she made a stop by a nearby oak tree to tie the knotted yarn around a branch without looking back.

After the third night, Granny Sue stopped by the young girl's home to check on her health status. The girl's fever had broken, and the color had returned to her cheeks. The mother extended her gratitude with a gift of homemade bread and some coins as payment. Granny Sue then set off again to tend to a laboring woman nearby.

The work is a blend of spiritual and natural worlds colliding to help those in dire need. In this healing system, a shared perspective on combatting sickness draws from the cultural exchange of African, European, and Indigenous practices—the wellness of the physical body is also a reflection of the spirit's health. In other words, if an individual's spirit is under attack, their physical body is also affected. Remedies employed by local healers include a few different measures to ensure that the body and spirit of the individual are well taken care of.

The work of healing doctors and medicine folk of all genders and ethnicities was vital to the common people's survival. Self-reliance, as we know, was at the forefront of everything the mountaineer did. That included finding solutions for sickness and maintaining good health. The mountain healer excelled in their knowledge of local flora, known by folklorists and the natural medicine world as *materia medica* and often recorded their wisdom in a book. The book would contain all their plant allies and included the native plant names, folk names, the plant's appearance, and corresponding treatments. The book also had recipes and formulas for tinctures, salves, and poultices. It served as a guide for facilitating their remedies to restore the body, mind, and spirit. This book would sometimes be inherited to help preserve the healing work of another. However, the best healers wouldn't need to reference their books at all. They stored all the important information in their noggin. You'd have to spend quality time with the healer in order to retrieve what they knew. Even then, some healers would only be able to provide vague descriptions of the plants they knew and folk nicknames rather than the formal Latin names. As long as they knew what they were talking about, it didn't matter much if you understood. This would lend itself to be tricky waters for those curious about the medicine practice of their elders. Further research would come in handy, and luckily, plenty of herbal books help fill in the gaps.

The generations that relied on their self-sufficiency were both stubborn and hesitant to break away from how they handled health-related issues with the rise of pharmaceutical methods. Old habits never truly died in this region. Local doctors and healers had their tried-and-true natural path of medicine and were already deeply part of the community. They were taught by fellow community members rather than going through an unfamiliar educational institution. They were well-trusted folks versus a stranger who is new to town. Plus, in some scenarios, there were a number of healers within the same family line. It became a generational practice, despite the rise of modern medicine. Doctoring, though it may not be as apparent today, continues to live on if you look close enough or know whom to ask.

DIAGNOSING THE SICK

Doctoring is straight to the point with herbal solutions and rites—no use in wasting precious time! In the rugged terrain, acting swiftly was crucial, whether tending to a sickly bedbound child, treating a bloody accident on the farm, or consoling a neighbor in emotional distress. The diagnosis process includes carefully listening to the client, observing their physical condition, and reading the signs from omens and divination to get a complete picture of potential threats. This allows the healer to come to a thoughtful diagnosis and offer a holistic solution.

By the Blood

Assessing an individual's overall well-being starts with their blood. Methods such as observing the color of urine or identifying a specific point on the body that refers to "where the water begins and where the blood ends" are utilized to gauge the quality of the blood and its cleanliness. This point indicates the individual's circulation and helps determine whether the client struggles with high or low blood, thick or thin blood, or, in African American folk healing practices, sweet or bitter blood. Some healers believed that this correlated with the shifts of the seasons and could help inspire which herbal preparations to make before the upcoming season.

High blood referred to folks who had high blood pressure. If someone was thought to have high blood, they were more prone to headaches, nausea, and nosebleeds. In this case, the healer would resort to some recorded remedies to attempt to "cut the blood." They'd brew tea concoctions like sassafras or recommend other remedies such as consuming certain pungent herbs and vegetables like onion and garlic.

If a person has *low blood*, they may experience health concerns such as fainting and dizziness from iron deficiency. This was more common during the winter months, when folks began to experience a shortage of fruits and vegetables. They'd rely on their preserves from the summer months to maintain a clean blood system, ensuring it remained steady until the spring. But if someone continued to struggle, the goal was to build the blood back up with tonics and thick sustenance, like molasses.

Traditional doctors and healers have their personal conclusions about the cause of sickness in the physical body. Clarence Gray, a local yarb doctor from West Virginia, was known for his spring tonic solutions to help "cut the blood" and purge the body, ensuring a deep cleanse for his clients. His practice and remedies originated from his lineage, with influence from a German family he worked for in Ohio, as well as the herbal knowledge of a Cherokee healer who helped him when he faced his own health concerns.

Gray believed that the blood could get "clogged" or too thick by eating certain types of foods, such as all the good stuff like coffee, pork, and potatoes. His tonic recipe contained herbs known to clean the blood and ones with laxative effects to encourage a purging process. This was a common approach to cleansing the body—what goes in must come out! This application encouraged a rebalance of the body's health. There was a fine line between it and self-inflicted poison approaches for purging. This was handled carefully to avoid misuse, and potentially causing more harm than good. Likewise, the same goes for individuals who may have struggled with thin blood, such as older folks who took longer to heal. The remedies provided by healers were crafted to help build the blood back up and included diets rich in fatty foods.

Gray was known for using bitters to cure diseases such as tuberculosis, black lung, and emphysema, all of which were severe diseases in this era with the working conditions in mines and factories. The specific formula would vary depending on what he could forage, but some essential plants were burdock, red clover roots, and peppermint.

The same goes for today, where modern healers pay close attention to their community's needs during different seasons and in people's personal lives. Natural remedies are still crafted by those who straddle contemporary and traditional herbal practices to protect the body during seasonal shifts. Based on their materia medica, the healer formulates a treatment for the sick and provides instructions for usage. The natural medicine crafted by the healer includes an array of bitters, salves, tonics, poultices, tinctures, and tea blends.

By the Body

A healer would assess an individual's physical state. Are they sweating from a fever? Are they pale in the face? Bleeding? Suffering heartburn? Like the contemporary doctor, they'd assess the person's physical pain, taking special notes to guide them through the diagnosis. The spread of physical illness was a familiar and feared reality. As more information came to light with the introduction to modern medicine, healers educated themselves on the various infections and diseases on the rise to continue serving their community. With this information on hand, they'd be able to identify the common illnesses based on the individual's physical well-being. Healers continued to play a crucial role in rural areas that remained untouched by contemporary medicine with their natural remedies to help combat and manage any illness outbreaks that swept through these isolated communities, such as tuberculosis, smallpox, typhoid fever, pneumonia, measles, and parasitic infections.

Many of these illnesses thrived on poor sanitation practices or contaminated water sources, or were seasonal during the winter months and were highly contagious. Unfortunately, this was the case for working-class households as housing structures and conditions began diminishing, particularly within coal camps. Plus, those responsible for the condition of the mines and factories had little to no regard for the lasting effects of health conditions. Workers were exposed to harsh environments, poor ventilation, and crowded living conditions. They were at constant risk from occupational hazards and the rapid spread of illness. The lack of affordable and accessible medical facilities meant that many outbreaks devastated entire communities. The local healer had a great responsibility to contain the spread of illness. They not only cured folks, but would also share their remedies with others along the way to provide common folk with more information to sustain themselves with plants found in their backyards.

We've witnessed something similar in our lifetime, having gone through collective attempts to contain coronavirus. The spread of this virus caused a global pandemic during which many people were quarantined in their homes and many died. Little was known about the virus when it first began circulating. It spread quickly, affecting many people's lives and health with lasting, long-term medical conditions. Where I lived at the time, a lot of misinformation spread about it. I can only imagine how our ancestors felt, experiencing many unfamiliar illnesses with little to no information available. Even with the amount of media access we have today, we were still left in the shadows of what was true and what wasn't.

I remember that as more information came to light and more people recovered from the virus, they shared natural remedies during their recovery process. Some had lost their sense of taste and smell. Various remedies were being shared on how people could recover them simply by using items from their kitchen cabinets. One of the methods I remember circulating was using burnt orange peels. You would char the orange, peel it, mash the warm pulp with sugar, and then eat it. The strong scent of the orange and the taste of burnt fruit would "reset" the smell/taste senses. It was a success for some, while others continued to search for alternatives. Still, it's an example of doctoring nonetheless, with folks teaching others in a public forum versus visiting one another's homes.

By the Signs and Omens

Besides treating an individual's physical symptoms as they were struggling with sickness, the healer would also resort to divination methods to further expand on *why* or *who* could be behind the illness. Local folklore describes the signs and omens to search for from the spiritual world. They served as indicators of a person's spiritual health. Simply paying attention to nature's signs could provide a quick answer when deciphering if other work was at hand.

This region has experienced an immense amount of death trauma, and the list is long when it comes to health omens and signs. There are many different approaches to reading the signs to diagnose a situation. The favored approach will vary with each practitioner. We'll focus on the most popular techniques for determining whether someone's spirit has been afflicted.

DREAMS

A personal favorite divination method of mine to deliberate a spiritual prognosis is through dreams. A lot can be revealed about a person's life based on their dreams. When our bodies enter REM sleep, our minds are more awake, and yet our bodies are still resting. This is when dreaming takes place.

In this liminal space, our spirit is able to communicate with us. Visuals and storylines begin to play out. Some folks have taught themselves to become active participants in their dreams—this is called *lucid dreaming*, and it's a practice that takes a lot of time and patience. Some herbs, like mugwort or passionflower tea blends, can assist. (Note: Mugwort can be unsafe for those who are pregnant, nursing, or trying to conceive, so it is best to steer clear of it if you are in one of those positions.) Another way to enhance your chances of dreaming comes from a Kentucky folk belief that placing a bone from a hog underneath your pillow will ensure a night of dreams (this was referred to as a *dream bone*).

My mother and I spent quality time interpreting each other's dreams. It is one of the ways we bonded. "I had a weird dream," she'd say, and we'd dig into it. Who was in it? What was happening? Where were you? Looking back, I can see that some of the earliest practices in my spiritual journey were incorporated at a young age from her. She had one of these dream interpretation dictionaries that I would eventually own myself. Before pulling the book out, we'd listen to each other describe in great detail what happened in our dreams, recovering everything we could before it disappeared from our minds. My mother always had some of the most vivid dreams. She would recognize faces and places and be able to reiterate them as if it were a movie she had just seen. I've always believed she was gifted with Sight, as she told me many stories of childhood dreams that would later unravel before her. In her dream state she would encounter spirits who had passed and who visited to communicate with her.

When interpreting dreams, the first thing is to pay close attention to the details and uncover as much as possible. I pay special attention to how the other person retells their dream. Are they in distress? Are they relieved? Emotions conveyed in the dream can be an important detail when assessing potential spiritual messages. Were they alone, or was someone there with them? Did they know who it was? If not, what was their association? Take special note of any presence of an individual. Lastly, consider the environment or setting of the dream. Was it somewhere familiar? Somewhere they've never been? What did it feel like to be there? Was it inside a building or outside in nature? It's like putting together a puzzle to determine what the spirits are conveying.

Other details and themes, such as animals, material possessions, or specific words and phrases that can be recalled, can provide some general context when interpreting dreams. Some old southern Appalachian folk beliefs about dreams include the following:

- To dream of a running hare means positive changes are ahead.

- To dream of an unbroken egg means trouble is coming.

- To dream of money is a sign of illness.

- If you tell a dream before breakfast, it will come true.

CARTOMANCY

Cartomancy, or divination using cards, is an old practice that has its history dabbling into the region as it became popularized between social classes. What was once a hushed practice, done behind closed doors or reserved only for the elite, later became more accessible by simply using a deck of playing cards. Folks gathered around playing card games is no unfamiliar scene, and the like applies to folk practitioners, too.

Every practitioner will have their preferred system, as several established systems from Europe have made their way over and are used in modern practices. We have the popular Rider-Waite tarot deck, which features seventy-eight cards divided into the major arcana, which consists of twenty-two cards, and the minor arcana, which consists of fifty-six cards and features the four different suits of wands, cups, pentacles, and swords. Then we have the Lenormand deck, composed of thirty-six cards with featured symbolic imagery corresponding to each card definition. Since playing cards were accessible and typically within almost every household, the divination practice translated into putting a mundane item to magical use. In a similar fashion to the Rider-Waite tarot system, each suit oversees a specific facet of life, such as actions, emotions, intellect, and physical/material matters. The pulled cards display a story for the practitioner to intuitively interpret for their client based on a traditional system and combining personal interpretations.

As a practitioner, cartomancy has become my preferred form of spirit communication when troubleshooting a possible spiritual infringement on an individual's circumstance. For my own interpretation of deciphering how to move forward with spiritual solutions, I use a combination of card systems for an in-depth picture. I find that the Lenormand deck delivers straightforward responses, whereas the Rider-Waite system allows for more complexity. More discreet practitioners have utilized playing cards for divination, as it can be seen as a card-playing game to the nonmagical eye.

OMENS

The natural world will find ways to communicate with the practitioner, and because we are in tune with the routines of animals and seasonal cycles, nothing unusual ever goes unnoticed. We recognize when a non-native bird visits our feeder. We see the alarm in having an abundance of random flies in an otherwise clean home. That's happened to me before. I noticed an odd amount of flies within the home even though the routine house care was handled. My family experienced an unexpected visit to the car mechanic, and my partner got physically ill, all followed by the abundance of flies— I'd kill one and three more would show up.

We'll explore superstitions and omens more later on, but we'll touch on some popular ones I grew up with here. Animals can sense the presence of another and have been referred to in different cultural traditions as messengers from the otherworld.

A black cat, for example, has become one of the most popular omens of bad luck if it crosses your path. To combat the bad luck, you'd pull a thread from your clothing and throw it in the same direction as the passing cat. A black cat crossing your path was also a sign of an upcoming accident. A practitioner on their way to perform a healing rite may be enticed to reschedule to avoid any mishaps. Or simply licking your finger and tracing a cross or "X" in front of you will help counter any bad luck on your way.

Birds flying into the home is also seen as a bad omen. I had this happen, too, in my mother's house years ago. We were preparing to watch a horror film when a crow suddenly busted into the main floor from the basement door. It was almost as terrifying as the film, which we turned off and watched another day. Should a bird fly into the home where the practitioner is tending, it would be a sign that something else may be at work. Especially if the bird was a crow, which has been seen as a death omen.

Growing up, I always associated owls with the mystical realm because of their keen eyesight, their ability to turn their heads 135 degrees on either side, and their nocturnal behavior. The sound of their hooting used to scare me as a kid. Traditionally, their hooting was an omen of disruption or an accident waiting to happen. Now, when I hear the hooting of an owl outside my altar window, I obtain further explanation of the forewarning with my Lenormand deck to decide whether to continue the intended working.

Such omens delivered by nature can signal to the healer and practitioner what may be at work here. Several different methods can be used to help identify the omen's significance. A common rule of thumb is to watch out for disturbances occurring three times. The first can sometimes be marked as a coincidence. The second allows for speculation to arise. The third is final confirmation that something, or someone, is at work here. This helps the healer determine the best way to move forward, whether that be an uncrossing spell, a return-to-sender spell, or otherwise.

FROM MAMAW'S BOOK OF SPELLS:
In Your Dreams

Note: Do not consume mugwort if you are pregnant, nursing, or looking to become pregnant. Ingest with caution. Always check with your physician before consuming herbal blends that may counter any prescription medications.

If I am in need of answers that require me to fly into the other realm, I turn to herbs and plants that can help induce dreaming. These plant spirits have been known to help seek guidance in the spirit world. One of such favored spirits is mugwort. This plant is considered a "witch herb," meaning it helps enhance the connection between our spirit and the others. Another important plant is valerian root. It is a calming root that helps ease our body to be more receptive in the dream world. Other plants that can be used are passionflower, blue lotus, and skullcap. A personal favorite blend includes mugwort, holy basil, rose, lavender, and chamomile.

To prepare this blend, add about ¼ tsp of each herb to a cup of hot water. Allow it to steep for about four minutes, then strain the blend. Add honey to taste. This is intended to be consumed before bed. An alternative is to add these herbs to a cloth bag and place it underneath your pillow.

As the tea is consumed, write what it is that you're hoping to gain on a piece of paper or in your personal journal: clarity or confirmation. Leave the journal or paper underneath your pillow as you drift off to sleep. Upon waking, take note on that paper or journal entry of any visuals or phrases that came forth during your slumber travels.

RITES BY THE HEALER

Repetition of any act continuously reinforces its potency. The more something is done, the more it affirms its effectiveness. Appalachians are known to repeat only practices that work and that closely tie into their own beliefs. Even without ever genuinely knowing its origin or the why behind it, if their Papaw or Mamaw did it, then so it is.

The act of passing through involves the afflicted person being cured by passing them through a natural formation, such as a hole in a boulder or a crooked tree branch. Natural formations, like a hole in a rock or a tree exhibiting an "unnatural" shape, were believed to possess magical abilities akin to those in the healing landscape. The passing-through rite wasn't done strictly in the natural landscape, as some would also pass a child between two people three times to heal them. The same goes for blessing an object to be used in healing. The object is passed through the smoke of an herbal blend with corresponding plants while reciting a prayer for the working.

The act of measuring involves an object, such as a stick or length of yarn, being measured to the individual's size. As soon as the person outgrew the object, they also outgrew the sickness. This was done to help heal illnesses such as asthma. A child would stand against a tree branch to be measured. The stick was then stored out of reach of the child. Once the child was grown, they would be cured of their asthma. The gnosis is that one could outgrow sickness just like their clothes.

The act of plugging was also done for healing. One would carve a hole into a living tree and then plug the hole with the afflicted individual's belongings. These could be personal items, such as their hair, or a piece of fabric, such as red flannel. The item is used as a tether from the person to the tree. The tree would then take on the sickness of the individual. But should anything happen to the tree, it would also happen to the person tied to it. This rite is commonly used to heal skin conditions such as warts.

Rub blood from the wart with a cloth and plug it into the tree's hole. The tree would then take on the wart and remove it from the individual. This was used by the Pennsylvania Dutch mountaineers who found themselves in the southern range, specifically for doctoring bewitchment. One would write a ticket with a Bible verse on a piece of paper. It would be plugged into a white oak tree using an iron rod. The iron rod would inflict pain on the witch who caused the individual's misfortune.

PRAYER

Prayer plays a big part in the rites by the southern healer. In the past, it was especially important for those who were deeply involved in their community church. Discovering my family's tradition of faith healing through specific prayers used by my grandfathers, who were pastors, has been challenging—mainly because evidence has yet to be uncovered. Though, I suspect in my bones that they applied these good words to those who needed them, one way or another.

Many folk practitioners who continue their ancestral practices were taught by someone within the family line who whispered prayers and practiced the ways behind closed doors. Not because they didn't want to help their neighbor—that goes against their values. It was because their relationship with Spirit was kept private and sacred. You never know who may overhear. An angry neighbor may find out how to counter their work if anyone outside their family learns of their prayers. It is better to be safe than sorry and recite the prayers within the mind or in a very low whisper.

In moments of need, I reference verses within the KJV Bible as I would any other magical source, seeking inspiration for components of a healing spell. The Book of Psalms is filled with incantations and prayers that can be applied in healing work. In moments of uncertainty, I like to leave it in the hands of my ancestral spirits to show me the prayer needed for what is being requested.

While sitting at my altar, I close my eyes with my hand on my child-hood Bible and state my inquiry, such as to heal a wound, to help ease the mind, to help aid an aching heart. . . . After focusing on this request, I flip the Bible open to wherever the spirits guide me. Regardless of the version, the Book of Psalms consistently occupies the Bible's center—a place I instinctively seek when needing guidance. With closed eyes, I let my finger roam the pages until it rests on a point. I open my eyes, and whatever verse my finger is pointed to is the one I work with. This practice is known as *bibliomancy*, and it can be used with other texts. Aside from the Bible, I like to use books of poetry as well. Poetry, in its own way, is a kind of prayer and I've found some spirits to prefer it.

Never underestimate the power of words. Prayer has become a favored remedy in workings of all kinds for me. A particularly helpful rite I will use for protection consists of showering and washing with an Epsom salt, olive oil, and rosemary scrub. While scrubbing from toe to head, recite Psalm 121:7–8: "The Lord shall preserve me from all evil: he shall preserve my soul. The Lord shall preserve my going out and my coming in from this time forth, and even for evermore." As an alternative to this prayer, I've written one that goes like this: "From my toes to my head, my spirit is cleansed and restored, protected by my wise and well ancestors, today and moving forward."

Another prayer I've used when accidentally burning myself by crafting candles on the stovetop is the one recorded from western North Carolina in 1939, found in Anthony Cavender's *Folk Medicine in Southern Appalachia*. To talk the burn out, like the burn whisperers are known to do, the prayer went like this: "God sent three angels coming from the East and West. One brought fire, another salt. Go out, fire, go in, salt. In the name of the Father, the Son, and the Holy Ghost." It's best to recite it three times with proper care of the burn to follow, like placing a potato slice over the affected area to help pull the burn out.

FOLK HEALING PUBLICATIONS

Aside from the knowledge passed down by Mamaw or Papaw, or the advice from other local healers, some publications emerged to educate common folk on home remedies. They enabled folks to become more self-sufficient and knowledgeable when it came to accessible home remedies. A degree in medicine wasn't needed for the common folk to treat themselves at home. All they would need was to be familiar with their local flora, which was the most natural relationship for the practitioner. Although regulated medicine and physicians arrived in the region, local folks were still prone to trusting their traditional folkways of natural medicine. The two primary books that surfaced and were in the hands of many households were *Gunn's Domestic Medicine* and *Long Lost Friend*.

Long Lost Friend by John George Hohman was a household staple. It's inspired by the practices of the Pennsylvania Dutch who settled in the northern region of Appalachia. The book was published in the 19th century and, even today, it plays a significant role as the first American grimoire with many folk remedies and faith healings that Appalachian families applied. The book itself is so prized that even possessing it was thought to ward off malevolency. Its contents are both medicinal and magical, a reflection of the work done by the common folk and practitioners, no matter their skillset or experience.

Meanwhile, physicians in the region began deterring folk remedies by enumerating their potential dangers. Hohman proposed that the book contained only tested and proven methods to revive the folkways. The collection includes herbal home remedies, prayers, and other spoken charms. It also served as a guide for those in rural areas, opening the path for anyone who desired to learn. This book allowed more accessibility to folk healing practices. Questions related to maintaining people's day-to-day lives, such as tending to their sick cattle, protecting against thieves, and avoiding an early death at the hands of their neighbor's gun, were answered with simple charms and prayers.

Similarly, *Gunn's Domestic Medicine*, also known as *Poor Man's Friend*, was another household item used in folk healing. With a lengthy list of healing remedies, *Gunn's Domestic Medicine* offered accessible solutions to the common folk in rural areas with limited health-care opportunities. John C. Gunn, an American physician, felt the call to empower the mountaineer by sharing medical knowledge for common illnesses without needing a visit from the physician. The text helped diagnose illness and advised on how to maintain good health. It was written in a way that was easy to understand and had practical solutions. Many of the book's remedies recommend a combination of healthy lifestyle practices to maintain overall holistic well-being. Whereas *Long Lost Friend* combined spiritual and medicinal, *Gunn's Domestic Medicine* was strictly medicine-focused. It empowered the people, who relied heavily on themselves and their limited resources, to manage their autonomy and take preventative care of their health.

With these two books, along with knowledge passed down from local yarb doctors and healers, the mountaineer was well-equipped with medicinal and magical remedies to tend the body, mind, and spirit. Today, with the increased knowledge and science behind modern medicine, many of these folk remedies are revived by those with a deep, profound connection to their land and generational traditions. As modern ways began to integrate, some old methods recorded only in books and by word of mouth became a thing of the past. However, there are still pockets in the rural communities where these traditions continue as a primary source of wellness. Though I was not raised solely on herbal medicine, I recognize how deeply rooted it is in the mountaineer's life and the animistic approach of the practitioner to building herbal relationships. Nature is medicine.

As a reminder, I am not a medical doctor who can provide recommendations for your health. Instead, this section is a means to highlight the ways of our Appalachian ancestors and acknowledge their tools and methods. I recommend consulting a physician or herbal healer for guidance if you are interested in practicing a natural-medicine path.

THE HEALING LANDSCAPE

The southern mountain region, with some of the oldest forests, serves as a perfect sanctuary for healing. The oak tree is a well-known provider in the dense woodlands region. The oak is associated with healing properties that traveled overseas and were instilled in the mountaineer's work. Its dense, large stature emphasized the tree's grandness. If lightning struck an oak tree, its healing properties would only increase. The tree branches would be collected for healing rites. Dogwood, a favorite of mine, is known for its local story of being used to make Jesus's cross. In return, the dogwood has a correspondence of protection and healing. The white and pink blossoms that emerge during the warmer months are a representation of the blood of Jesus, furthering its association with miracle work. The pine is also a guardian of the Appalachian forests. In Cherokee lore, it is tied to resilience during the harshest weather conditions. It is among the few trees that withstand the winter's long slumber. It is also a tree spirit that can be used in healing rites, with pine needles brewed as tea concoctions or used for smoke cleansing the home.

Another noteworthy healing tree is sassafras. This shrub is sacred medicine in the region and is frequently applied in southern magical practices. The Cherokee viewed sassafras in its entirety as a beacon of light for healing. Every ounce of the tree was used when foraged, from the roots to the leaves. After the discovery of its medicinal potency, it was incredibly sought after overseas. With its success in safely arriving during overseas transportation, folks began to associate sassafras beyond its medicinal healing properties. In folk charms, sassafras is used in magical workings such as success in business, wealth sustainability, and money luck. It is also used for protection and healing charms.

The winding rivers served as a fruitful landscape for seeking counsel and cleansing. Local rivers were frequently designated spaces for dedicated rituals regarding counsel, healing, and cleansing. For the Cherokee, specific rivers and lakes held powerful enchantments believed to cleanse and heal the spirit in river ceremonies. The Scots-Irish immigrants carried similar traditions in water's magical potency, drawn to sacred wells and rivers where they prayed and gathered water for charms. In this cultural intersection, water is a bridge between the physical and spiritual realms, offering renewal and healing. The practice of turning to a body of water for healing and cleansing integrated into the Christian framework in the form of baptisms. One would be walked to the river with the local pastor and church attendees to witness the cleansing rite.

Now, I mention the magical potency of the elements water and earth for a particular reason. Combine the magic of the tree and water, and you get stumpwater. Stumpwater is captured rain in its purest form, delivered straight from the sky and blessed by the tree spirit. Depending on the type of tree, stumpwater is used to determine a charm's success. Oak is a fine spirit when it comes to removing any skin illnesses. Stumpwater from oak was something a wart doctor preferred to use for its strength and effectiveness. Gathering stumpwater was also helpful in other areas of healing, such as curing other skin conditions like acne or rashes. Back in the day, when freckles were considered "hideous marks," stumpwater was the solution for wiping them away. My Mamaw told me growing up that my freckles were simply "kisses from angels," so I never sought out oak stumpwater. It can also be used in sprays to help restore and rejuvenate the skin. Early practitioners and healers collected stumpwater by absorbing it with a handy rag to wring out later for their workings and ailments. It's said that collecting stumpwater is best to do on Thursdays and in private. Refrain from talking to anyone about your whereabouts when you go collecting.

I have also found that it is excellent for scrying. I'll first collect the stumpwater and then pour it into a bowl. I will gaze into the water by candlelight and take note of any visuals that come through in the stumpwater's reflection. Having a notebook nearby is handy for reflecting on the findings after the divination session.

HERBAL ALLIES

The native flora that flourished in the mountaineer's backyard was a natural gift when diseases began to arise. Plants provided aid for the sickness of mind, body, and spirit. The *doctrine of signatures* correlates the medicinal use of a plant directly with its physical appearance. The common folk names of plants also correlated with their medicinal properties. A favorite wildflower commonly found in the Appalachian region and in the Pacific Northwest is violets. Violets, nicknamed heart's ease, lend themselves to be a cure for matters of the heart with the top flower resembling heart lobes. This plant was crafted into a tonic and prescribed to strengthen the heart. With this in mind when it comes to further herbal research, referencing the look of a particular plant can provide clues and hints to the beginner herbalist about medicinal and magical properties.

Exploring the local and ancestral folklore of a plant unveils a wealth of knowledge and inspiration for practitioners seeking to connect with the plant's spirit. These tales stemming from Indigenous, African, and European roots provide more than mere cultural insight; they also act as living guides, hinting at a plant's potential, both spiritual and medicinal. Regional stories in the southern Appalachian mountains remind us that plants are not just ingredients but rather the essence of a place, embodying its unique wisdom. The narratives of each plant offer a framework that the practitioner can apply in their magical workings. By reading these stories, we're able to approach plant spirits in a way that feels authentic and meaningful.

Popular Mountaineer Herbal Allies

Note: It is worth mentioning that when incorporating herbal remedies, it is your responsibility to explore beyond this book and to work alongside a physician for safety reasons.

What follows is by no means a complete list of the herbal allies that the healer and practitioner will encounter in the vast mountain region. I selected a handful that I am most familiar with and have found fascinating.

Several approaches prove beneficial when acquainting oneself with bioregional plants. Building a spiritual relationship with these plants takes time and observation across all seasons. Documenting their appearances throughout the year, from summer to winter, helps us understand their unique behaviors and how best to integrate them into herbal and magical solutions.

As stewards of the land, it is essential to adhere to regional laws governing wildcrafting, the practice of harvesting local plants for personal use. Checking local regulations and endangered species lists is crucial, as overharvesting can harm ecosystems and jeopardize plant populations, as seen in the case of ginseng. Approach foraging with mindfulness and ethical consideration. If there is an opportunity to learn from a local herbal mentor, I recommend it. The hands-on guidance can be a beneficial experience beyond what's available in books.

Take the time to get to know each plant, starting in your backyard or the local park. Really immerse yourself in learning about the plant and identifying the spirit's characteristics. Approaching this with mindfulness and the purest of intentions will be well received. We should remind ourselves of the interconnectedness between ourselves and nature, often reflecting upon each other. What may be present in our lives may be mirrored in the plants that begin to make themselves more known. I have found this to be true on my journey. When I first moved to the Pacific Northwest and was grieving the loss of my home in the mountains, I discovered an abundance of yarrow in my neighborhood. I recognized that this plant spirit presented itself as a guide during this chapter of my life. I recommend recording such experiences to reflect on later.

BLACKBERRY | RUBUS FRUTICOSUS

I've shared the story of my summers spent harvesting the ripe blackberries abundant in the higher elevations of the Blue Ridge Mountains. Their magical and medicinal usage extends beyond scrumptious summer berry pies. When hiking through dense forests, one encounters these tangled shrubs that ambitiously extend and quickly overtake their surroundings, creating thick mazes of slender vines. Adorned with thorns that grasp even the smallest flannel fibers, they invite you into their wooded maze. Flowers blossom in white and pink, with deep plum-colored berries in their prime.

The naturally arched hedges were considered liminal spaces for magical healing rituals and portals to the otherworld. They are another enchanting landmark in nature used in passing-through rites or to stand within for spirit communion. A folk healing remedy for the sick involves passing the afflicted person through the arched hedge to become healthy again, reflecting the healing rite of passing.

In herbal medicine, the blackberry is an antioxidant that cleanses the body and nurtures the liver. Tinctures can be crafted from the leaves to treat skin irritations. The Cherokee would strip the bark and leaves to use in teas to treat an upset stomach. The berries aided in building the blood to prepare for the winter months with enriched nutrients such as iron and vitamin C. The berries can also be used to make beverages, such as wine and brandy, to warm the body and build blood.

The blackberry is also tied to the dead and is often positioned in grave-yards to keep wandering spirits from haunting the grounds. A protection charm from the British Isles mentions the usage of bramble leaves infused in a floor wash to ward against ill-intended spirits. I like using the thorned branches of the blackberry to capture unwanted energy from the home, then I bury the branches far away to dissolve the energy.

Lastly, the blackberry bush is also associated with the devil, as the figure was cast away from the heavens and landed in a blackberry bush. Out of frustration, the devil turned the blackberry bush to taste bitter and sour. With this story, practitioners and healers would avoid harvesting from the blackberry bush after Michaelmas in September, the day which also cor-relates to when the devil cursed the blackberries. Consuming blackberries or harvesting before Michaelmas was done to avoid misfortune.

BURDOCK | ARCTIUM LAPPA AND A. MINUS

The English, French, and Dutch brought with them a handful of seeds into Appalachia, and burdock was one of them. It settled in and is naturalized, making a home in open fields around the mountain valleys with damp soil and meadows. The plant's tall frame supports a thorny crown with purple flowers and long, coarse, almost heart-shaped leaves. After their prime in the late summer and early fall, the crowns begin to dry, making it easy for the bur to latch onto clothing with its tiny teeth. The plant is steeped in folklore across Europe. In Cornwall, the tufts that covered old fields were thought to be horses' hair, evidence of faeries riding at night.

Yarb doctors and rootworkers were familiar with applying burdock in cleansing the blood and restoring one's health. Rootworkers specifically soaked the roots in whiskey to combat unfamiliar illnesses. Its leaves were crafted into a salve recipe mixed with animal fat to help soothe skin irritations and promote healing from cuts.

Due to the plant's medicinal use to cleanse the blood and restore health, practitioners can use it for cleansing and protection magic. This extends to an old charm made of seeds being strung together as a home protection charm that would prevent intruders. When the plant is dry, the burs can be used in protection charms to ward off unwanted energy with their spikes. Carefully collect enough to store in the corners of your home for any undesirable spirits or energy to be caught by the plant's teeth.

GINSENG | PANAX QUINQUEFOLIUS

An essential root in Appalachian herbal medicine, ginseng is on the brink of extinction. The physical body of this plant is distinctive and has similarities to the legendary European mandrake root. Though not from the same family, they both include a fleshy body representing a human body with "legs" formed at the root by their forked branches. Above the ground, the plant consists of five leaflets arranged in a spiral atop a central stem. White flowers bloom during the warmer months, and the autumn season delivers its nutritious red berries.

The Cherokee used this plant in their healing remedies, which they taught their new neighbors. In their healing practices, teas and tonics are crafted with this plant to restore balance and harmony by "cooling down" the body. It helped treat symptoms of arthritis and ease headaches.

By acknowledging ginseng's nourishing qualities, mountaineers held the plant in high regard. Its medicinal value intrigued commercial interest from other countries, leading to a surge in digging up the root to sell for a pretty penny. *Sangin'* is what locals would say to reference going out and harvesting this plant. It became a family fall tradition to go digging in the woods and hunt down an abundance to harvest. In the 18th century, farmers began cultivating secret patches on their own homesteads, closely guarding their lot with a promise of good fortune. Despite the mountaineers' deep connection to the land, some faced heavy financial hardship and resorted to overharvesting and selling it to overseas markets to support their families.

Ginseng remains an important part of Appalachia's agricultural history and culture. The admiration went so deep that it nearly took the plant's life away for good. Its history of assisting a family's financial situation demonstrates that it can also be used for money workings. Ginseng's recovery is a long one. To protect and revive it, strict harvesting laws have been applied. A best practice is to take only what you need and leave the rest alone.

JUNIPER | JUNIPERUS

Juniper is a strong shrub that is used in landscaping to create thick property

barriers. Its blue-purple berries ripen during the fall and early winter. Juniper is mainly known for its use in gin making, and it is accompanied by other spices for a delicate taste. Medicinally, the berries can be used to help with digestive issues.

Magically, juniper is a plant whose association crosses over into various cultures. The Cherokee recognized juniper as one of their beloved allies to smoke cleanse individuals and spaces. In British Isles traditions, the Scottish would scatter sprigs of juniper around their cattle to prevent bewitchment and employ the plant spirit for protection. With the shrub's thick structure, juniper is known to be the gateway into the spiritual realm. It sometimes is planted around graveyards and properties to protect the spirits within. In a similar way, juniper branches can be used for protection charms.

MULLEIN | VERBASCUM THAPSUS

Displayed abundantly along the roadside, in open fields, and crawling up hillsides, mullein can be found reaching high in the sky during the summer and early fall days. The plant presents a tall, spear-like shape adorned in yellow honey-scented blossoms under the late Sun's warmth. The leaves extend largely low to the ground and near the base of the stem. Though not native to this soil (it was brought over by European settlers), it became an effective plant for all to use in their healing remedies.

Mullein tea can be used medicinally to treat sore throats and chest coughs. The downy leaves are soaked in water and crafted into a poultice for swollen joints and sore muscles.

Before they depart back into winter's slumber, I harvest a few mullein stalks for personal crafting. With mullein being associated with warding off the evil spirits of the night, it can be used magically as protection charms and guardians of the home. With the few I've gathered, I enchant them and place them near my windowsill as a guard against energetic infiltrations during the late summer and early autumn days.

Before the use of cotton, the fibers of mullein were used for lamp wicks, leading to one of its folk names, candlewick plant. In English superstitions, witches supposedly used lamps and candles with wicks made from mullein to ride to their sabbats at night. This is how the other folk name of hag's taper was born. Should you decide to craft mullein into candles for ritual purposes, it is best to keep an eye on them, as they can ignite quite powerfully—and never leave a lit candle unattended.

SASSAFRAS | SASSAFRAS ALBIDUM

I've mentioned sassafras before regarding healing remedies, but I would be remiss if I didn't expand further. This small tree consists of skinny orange-

brown branches with leaves that remind me of the shape of a duck's feet. During the tree's prime, small flowers bloom a yellow star with a hint of lime green. The roots are substantial and woody, with a soft bark that is either reddish or brown in color. Once the flowers fall, berries that taste like cinnamon are present in the cooler months.

The Cherokee thought highly of the sassafras tree. It was yet another ally in their apothecary cabinet. The inner white bark of the tree's branches was used as a cure-all remedy as it is a blood purifier. It was also crafted into a tonic to cure a restless spirit and body and tend to those with weak hearts.

Sassafras is a key ingredient in spring tonics. Along with spicebush and sweet birch, it forms the potent S.S.S. Tonic. The twigs and root bark can be used as tea or jelly, while the leaves are dried for soup dishes. It gained momentum in the root-digging industry for its role in curing stomach pain, eye inflammation, and fever. It helped strengthen the heart and was known to support overall good health. An old mountain saying that advocated for the plant's use can be found in *Smokehouse Ham, Spoon Bread, and Scuppernong Wine* by Joe Dabney, which includes the southern hill-country food and lore:

In the spring of the year,
When the blood is too thick,
There is nothing so fine
As a sassafras stick.
It tones up the liver,
And strengthens the heart,
And to the whole system
New life doth impart.

It was also used for other culinary purposes. A recipe shared in the Foxfire series was to make candy out of sassafras by grating the bark, boiling and straining it, then pouring it into boiling sugar to harden. Break into pieces, and enjoy. Making homemade root beer was also a cherished springtime tradition in many Southern homes. The roots were harvested, stripped, and boiled to create a concentrated tea. This concentrate was then mixed with water, chilled, and served over ice. The roots could be reused for another batch since their flavor lasts.

If you are considering making sassafras tea or consuming products made from sassafras root, it is important to be aware of potential health risks. Sassafras was famously used in commercial root beer recipes until the FDA banned the ingredient in the 1970s because it contains safrole, a known carcinogen.

In folk magic, the root is employed to draw in wealth by placing it in personal items like wallets. In the mountains of North Carolina, it was carried as a charm to protect one's overall well-being. Burning sassafras inside the home was discouraged as it was an omen to an early family death or would bring illness.

STINGING NETTLE | URTICA DIOICA

My partner once told me how he used to get pricked by nettle growing up in the countryside of England. But nature has a funny way of delivering a solution in close proximity to harm. Nettle often grows beside burdock, which can be used to alleviate the sting by crushing the leaves and placing them on the wound. Due to its crude nature in causing skin irritation and burning, stinging nettle has acquired quite a few nicknames, such as the devil's beard. If you're not accustomed to this stinging sensation, I highly recommend wearing gloves when working with nettle. As part of the initiation into working with this spirit, I have found you are bound to experience its wrath at least once or twice.

Nettle is a nutritious plant and can be served in salads or other dishes prepared with a little bit of salt, garlic, and butter. Teas were also crafted to help with inflammation and heal the liver. The Scots-Irish would make fiber from the nettle plant to produce fabric for garments and other household needs. Folks also used nettle to dye their yarn, as the plant produces a muted red color.

Magically, it is associated with workings related to healing, protection, and binding. It is also tied to devil lore found in the Isle of Skye that identified May third as the day the devil was sent down from the heavens, and nettle grew where he landed, similar to the blackberry story. Apparently, the devil figure often finds himself tangled in plants that sting and poke.

The tie between this plant and the devil spirit can be an inspiration to use nettle to evoke the folkloric figure. It has also been employed in healing rites. A relative of the sick would grasp ahold of the plant with their bare hands, enduring its pain, while chanting the name of the sick person to help cure them.

OLD WAY HEALING REMEDIES

The following examples shed light on traditional folk healing methods and offer insights into the contents of historical folk healing publications during the 19th and 20th centuries prior to contemporary medicine. While some of these remedies may still be practiced in households, others serve as intriguing records of the past. It's important to approach these with caution and observation rather than immediate application.

FOR THE HEAD

- To cure a headache, tie a red cloth around the head. Or try drinking water from a springwater creek running east to west before sunrise.

- You can also try praying a headache away. Repeat the prayer thrice, "Tame thou flesh and blood like Christ in paradise who will assist thee, this I tell [state name], for your repentance-sake." Allow three minutes before stating it every minute until the headache ceases.

- Never let a bird take a hair from your head to make its nest, as it will result in a headache. Likewise, never break a bird's nest.

FOR THE CHEST

- To lessen a cough, combine the juice of garlic and honey and take by the spoonful.

- Or create an onion poultice by slicing and drying onions, combining with hog lard, and binding with cornmeal. Fill a red flannel cloth with the mixture, avoiding direct contact with the skin. Place the poultice on the chest.

- Make a cough syrup with wild cherry bark, honey, sugar, and mullein leaves.

- To sweat a cold out of the body, brew a tea of dried mullein and boneset leaves.

FOR THE STOMACH

- To treat diarrhea, make tea from blackberry root or drink wine made from the fruit.

- For constipation, rub castor oil on the stomach and back to get the intestines moving.

- To help with indigestion, chew goldenseal root or boil in a tea.

- To prevent nausea, brew a cup of catnip tea. This was used specifically for pregnant women.

- An onion a day keeps the doctor away! Oh, and an apple. Maybe not together, though.

FOR THE BLOOD

- Eat garlic and onions to keep the blood clean come spring.

- To stop a nosebleed, tie a woolen string around your left thumb. Or try brewing a pot of nettle tea.

- To stop the blood from a wound, recite Ezekiel 16:6.

FOR THE SKIN

- To heal burns and cuts, make a salve using the flower, leaves, and stems of the yarrow plant.

- To whisper a burn away, say, "Burn, I blow on thee!" and blow on it three times in the same breath.

- To cure a bruise, speak the prayer: "Bruise, thou shalt not heat; bruise, thou shalt not sweat; bruise, thou shalt not run, no more than Virgin Mary shall bring forth another son." Or try making a poultice from plantain leaves.

- Pick a wart with a sanitized pin, then bury the pin at a crossroads.

DOWN THE RABBIT HOLE
Midwifery

In the health-care landscape, local women were compassionate souls who tended to other women's health, specifically taking on the role of a midwife. To be someone who tends to another in the space of welcoming new life takes a special kind of soul. The same goes for caretakers tending to older folks leaving this realm and moving on to whatever is next. Women have played these roles throughout the region's history. However, I want to state that these caretaking positions are not gender-specific roles today.

During childbirth, women would invite other women within the family and of kin to help them during this transition. They would not only aid the new mother during birth, but also in matters such as tending the home, preparing meals, and helping with other children in the household. Their skill in facilitating the transformation in the birthing room was taught by those with experience in the area. For centuries, and even today, childbirth is an incredible transformational experience for both mother and child. The correlation between a new soul entering the physical realm and the birth of a new identity for the mother requires a special kind of guide with keen understanding to usher in this new phase with compassion and care.

Midwifery continues well into the 21st century, not only for accessibility purposes but also for emotional support. When physicians entered the rural region, many were expensive and financially inaccessible to many families. On the other hand, midwives offered their services for the sake of being on good terms with their neighbors and to continue a generational practice. If they were to exchange their skills for monetary value at all, it would be for a fraction of what the doctor in the next town over would charge. Their services were not with money in mind but rather ensuring the lives of women and children were safe in the hands of someone who knew a thing or two.

Some women became so dedicated to increasing safe and accessible resources for child-bearing folks in the mountains that they decided to further their efforts in obtaining higher education. Mary Breckinridge was one of the women who believed in reforming the medical landscape for midwifery and children. She volunteered as a nurse during World War I, returning to America to continue her medical education. She then took her studies abroad to England, aiming to gain certification in rural midwifery. Upon completing her studies, she applied her knowledge to establish the Kentucky Committee for Mothers and Babies. This would grow and transition into the Frontier Nursing Service to increase accessibility for public health services in Leslie County, Kentucky. In due course, the organization evolved into Kentucky's inaugural nursing university by 1928. This development enhanced women's health care within the health system, promoting safety and improvement in rural towns.

Whether they were midwives or not, grannies always had a cure with something up their sleeves or in their cabinets. Stored in their kitchen apothecaries were elderberry syrups for the chest, tea blends to ease aches and pains, and broths to warm the body during cold winter nights. The best of it all was that sometimes the cure was just a gentle squeeze on the hand or a humbling hug during grievances. These friendships with one another were strong and remind us all that sometimes the best medicine is each others' company.

FROM MAMAW'S BOOK OF SPELLS:
Wade Away the Worry

When it comes to healing, water is a treasured spirit. Bodies of water have always brought me peace during tumultuous seasons of my life. Around these hills are rivers and lakes hidden behind thick rhododendrons in the summer and exposed during autumn and winter.

When in need of emotional healing, visit a local river as the Sun begins to set during the warmer months and immerse yourself in it. While wading, recite Isaiah 43:2 or this prayer I've written:

> *Water of [name of the body of water],*
> *May your spirit flow through me and over my body.*
> *From the veins of this river,*
> *Of the Earth's blood,*
> *May my aches and pains be swept away*
> *By the gentleness of you.*

Repeat as many times as feels right to you. You may also speak your worries directly to the water, allowing them to be washed away down the river. You can bring along a mason jar to gather the river water for cleansing work, too. Take it home with you and store it securely. Be sure to label and date the water. I like to dampen a cloth with the water to wash my hands before a working for a friend or community member to ensure my hands are cleansed from energy that may interfere. You may also use it for washing your floors and thresholds during home-cleansing rituals.

FROM MAMAW'S BOOK OF SPELLS:
Protect These Walls Powder

For this protection powder, you will need:

- Myrrh
- Frankincense
- Dried cedar
- Cinnamon bark
- Mortar and pestle

First, gather all your materials near your mortar and pestle. Begin with the myrrh and grind it into a fine powder. Then add the frankincense, grinding it into a fine powder with the myrrh. Continue placing the dried cedar and cinnamon bark into the blend, grinding it until it is a fine powder.

This powder can be placed along windowsills and in doorways, or be used in an oil to anoint protection candles.

FROM MAMAW'S BOOK OF SPELLS:
Healing Salve

For this salve, you will need:

- Infused chamomile oil:
  - » Mason jar
  - » Dried chamomile
  - » Olive oil
- Beeswax
- Tin container with lid

Begin by making your infused chamomile oil under a Full Moon. With your mason jar, fill it about halfway with the dried chamomile. Add enough olive oil to cover the chamomile and reach just below the top of the mason jar. Secure the lid, and label and date the jar. Infuse the oil for an entire Full Moon cycle, about twenty-eight days, periodically shaking the infusion. Strain the infused oil under the next Full Moon into a clean mason jar, and label and date it. Store the infused oil in a cool place until you're ready to use it.

For the salve, in a double boiler, melt the beeswax. Add the infused oil in a 2:1 ratio—so two parts beeswax to one part oil—and stir. Pour the infused beeswax into the tin container and set it aside to cool and solidify. Then put the lid on and store in a cool place.

Use this salve when you intend to do healing work by adding some to the palms of your clean hands and rubbing gently together.

6

A TALE WORTH TELLING:
EXPLORING SOUTHERN APPALACHIAN
SUPERSTITIONS, SPIRITS, AND OMENS

My mother often spoke about her ghostly encounters growing up. These experiences were normalized and weren't necessarily shared to instill fear in me or anything like that. Sometimes, if I'm being truthful, I didn't always believe her. I believed in fairy tales and whatnot, but ghosts were unknown and apparently only present at night. Those speculations quickly went out the door when I was ten years old.

My first experience with a spirit interaction was at my mother's house in Flat Rock, North Carolina. It wasn't a very old house and didn't appear to have any "red flags." It looked very typical from the outside, nestled in a quaint neighborhood. It was just a one-story 1970s ranch-style home that looked like the others. The yard was nice but not too big, with neighboring houses around. I remember taking note of the well that was in the backyard. For some reason, it always gave me the creeps.

One night, as I was going to bed in the room shared with my baby sister, who wasn't even a year old at the time, I overheard several people talking just outside the window. I couldn't tell where the voices were coming from. I peeked into the dark to see if the neighbors were in their backyard having a party, but I couldn't see anyone. Besides, we lived in a quiet neighborhood where hardly any activity happened. Sometimes I'd catch a word clearly, as if the voices were speaking right next to me. This only confused me even more. Other times, the voices were distant and muffled. Who was talking? Where were they coming from?

These voices kept me up on the nights I heard them, and I became tired and irritable by the constant chatter. I'd wake up and complain to my mother that either the television was too loud or I could hear her talk all the way from the back of the house. That was the only way I could make sense of the voices. Her face would be perplexed when I complained in the morning, but she was never concerned. She moved me to her quilting room to try and sleep there with the radio on to help drown out the noise, but it never worked. Instead, it would be even more distracting, and I'd become more tired.

One evening, we were gathered in the family room when a heavy plastic container of sewing material in the back room crashed to the ground. It startled all of us, and we joked about a ghost being present. I remember feeling afraid and unsure and wondered if perhaps being in the quilting room wasn't any better for me. Afterward, I decided to move back into the shared bedroom.

I prayed that the voices would finally spare me. But the murmuring continued. I was becoming engulfed in aggravation. After not being able to get another solid night's rest, I became an entirely different person. One night, I made my way into the living room, crying from exhaustion. With the television remote in my hand, I begged the voices to stop talking and threw the remote at my mother's bedroom door. She had been fast asleep and jolted awake, rushing out of her bedroom only to see me crying in the hallway.

It wasn't long before I moved from the Flat Rock home and into my father's house for the new school year. My mother had shared with me her own experience that later confirmed my ghostly suspicions. One night, she went to check on my crying sister, and she looked up at the window above her crib. This window was high off the ground and would only be accessible if someone was about ten feet tall. But that night, she looked up at the window and saw a shadowed figure looking in. She said something overcame her in that moment. She placed my sister back down into her crib, walked back into the bedroom, lay down, and folded her arms across her chest to immediately go back to sleep. She said it felt like something had "possessed" her to do so or enchanted her in some way. That's when it was decided that it was time to move out of the house.

Being invited to a neighbor's cookout or to sit on their front porch overlooking the hills with a fresh glass of sweet tea in hand is a scene for storytelling. There is no grand audience witnessing Mamaw talk about the faeries in her garden or Uncle John swearing he saw a haint on his recent hunting trip. It's an intimate exchange among trusted kin. One person spills the beans on what they've been told while the others listen closely, wondering if it's just a load of hocus-pocus shenanigans. The air is rather humid, the mountains are smoky, the local cardinals appear vivid against the dipping sunlight, and local stories of ghosts and land spirits are exchanged. If nobody truly wanted to learn about the haints, spirits, or what have you, then perhaps they'd choose to keep quiet altogether. But people love a good ole gossip, no matter who the characters are.

The tradition of storytelling reflects the exchanges that adapted into the present Southern mountain culture. Telling stories has always been about having a good time as much as passing the time. There was sure to be banter with Southern humor and dialects that outsiders wouldn't always know how to interpret. Some stories had an antagonist (hero) versus a protagonist (trickster). Others were meant to explain the natural world, the supernatural, and everyday life. These narratives often embodied community values such as family loyalty and justice, as told in feud tales. They sometimes hinted at shared feelings and experiences that would unite the people. Exchanging stories breathes life into the past and helps explain how we came to adopt superstitions. With every share, we take away something new.

The preservation of folklore is heavily dependent on this front porch tradition. It acts as a thread that ties us to the past of our people and the land we call home. It serves as a compass, guiding practitioners who reference folktales to help with ancestral veneration and developing an intimate connection with local spirits. Storytelling is the magic that shines light on our shared human experiences and illuminates the complexities of our collective journey. Oral tradition reminds us that nothing will ever truly be forgotten if we continue doing exactly what we're doing right now—sharing stories.

But what exactly constitutes a folktale? How long does it take to integrate into a community or group of people? Is it possible for new stories to emerge and flourish? I personally think so. Consider the stories you are being told today. Perhaps they are adaptations of earlier stories designed to fit into the present world. They may be fresh in some respects, but an older tale can often inspire the framework.

In this chapter, I had the pleasure of recording some folk stories directly from the mountain, even from afar. I wish I had gathered more, and perhaps in due time that'll come. But for now, I wanted to capture the stories before they were lost. You will also hear some retold stories that I've heard growing up. In addition, I'll share a little about the superstitions from this place, but know that it is not the entire collection. Those books have already been written, with new collections printed in due time.

I find that superstitions have been unconsciously applied in my daily life when they make sense because, if you didn't know, I'm somewhat superstitious. If my mother were here right now, she'd make a smart remark about superstitions, alluding to the impression that sometimes superstitions don't make much sense. This is ironic, because she is very superstitious, whether she recognizes it or not. *Don't call attention to it, you'll speak it into existence. Knock on wood. Hold your breath as we pass by the cemetery. Hold your breath while we pass through the tunnel.* It may seem silly to the outsider, but I simply can't help myself.

STORIES FROM THE SOUTHERN MOUNTAIN

A Retelling of "Jack and the Devil"

The tales of Jack are familiar ones in the South. The main character, Jack, takes on various roles, and how he is perceived depends on who's telling the story. His role is either that of a young boy on adventurous journeys or of an older gentleman who is incredibly bitter, among many other characters. But who is Jack, really? Well, the name goes back to British storytellers across the pond. "Jack" was used as a general name so that the teller wouldn't have to think too hard to make one up every time a new story was told. It's similar to John Doe when the story isn't really speaking of anyone specific.

It was a common name to use in stories over and over again, and turned into an entire series known as *Jack Tales*. The oral tradition of these British stories integrated well into the South as Jack's character changed to apply to the American people. The stories of Jack were shared around dinner tables to entertain guests or before bedtime to teach lessons to the young. What comes to mind when you hear the name "Jack" in reference to a story? For me, it's "Jack and the Giant Peach," or "Jack and the Beanstalk," like mentioned earlier, or the popular variety tales of "Jack and the Devil."

I like this story of "Jack and the Devil" around the autumn season because it relates to the popular tradition of pumpkin carving. In this story, Jack's character is a bitter man. He was found guilty of absurd behavior and was incredibly rude to the neighbors, children, and anybody, really. Nobody was exempted from his spite. You'd find him socializing at the local pub, bantering and gambling away his money. He wasn't nice to the local kids and cared little about anybody but himself. Jack, and his unsettling behavior, embodied every characteristic we're wary of. Some people would even consider him the devil himself in human form.

Despite his bitter soul, Jack was a farmer with a knack for growing the finest apples in town. Coming from a hometown surrounded by apple orchards, I can vouch that once you stumble upon a gem of an apple farm, you're always going there and nowhere else. That's what Jack's apples were to the locals—the go-to spot for the juiciest fruits, perfect for whipping up jams and pies that'd make your mouth water. Jack's apples were something else, so good that even the devil himself caught wind of their reputation. The devil decided to visit the earthly realm just to snag a few.

One day, the devil appears on Jack's doorstep, craving those renowned apples. Jack leads him to an apple tree, where the devil becomes so captivated by the luscious fruit that he doesn't notice Jack carving a cross into the tree stump where the devil had climbed. The devil finds himself stuck at the top of the apple tree, all thanks to Jack's quick thinking. With a grin, Jack leaves the devil stranded, feeling pretty pleased with himself for outsmarting the devil.

Eventually, that bitterness consumed him, leading to his demise. When he reached the gates of heaven, an angel turned him away. Some versions say it was Saint Peter himself who denied his entry. Jack's cruel ways in life didn't earn him a spot beyond the pearly gates. Confused and taken aback, Jack found himself redirected down below, where the devil held court. But once Jack had left the physical realm, the charm of the cross carved into the apple tree where the devil remained had also vanished, and the devil returned to his reign.

You'd think such a cruel spirit like Jack would be welcomed in hell, but not even the devil wanted him. He also turned Jack away, proclaiming that he will linger in darkness forever. Jack, now roaming the in-between realm, was considered a lost soul. All around him was darkness. But the devil did do him one little favor and kicked over a piece of hot coal. With the coal's illuminating light, Jack discovered a pumpkin nearby that he picked up to carve into. (Now, in some variations of this story, he used a turnip that was stored in his pants pocket. This old tale was brought over from the Scottish and Irish, who didn't have pumpkins in their native land, reflecting the story's British origins.) He made himself a lantern with the piece of glowing coal and carved vegetable. Now he's forever roaming as Jack, the lost soul.

I've never seen the wandering spirit myself, though I had my fair share of suspicions late at night during camping season, only to be proved later that it was a neighboring camper instead. During the fall season, I partake in pumpkin carving, a tradition meant to fend off spirits like Jack during the darker months and on Halloween.

Helen's Bridge and Zealandia:
Buncombe County, North Carolina

I first encountered Helen's Bridge in high school, when I followed my curiosity about local tales and haunted spots. I'm no paranormal investigator; I respectfully engage with spirits by reading their stories from afar. Occasionally, however, I'm drawn to places with intriguing tales that stir courage in my heart to witness the story's origin firsthand. In the case of Helen's Bridge, I felt a profound sadness for Helen and the story that forever bound her to that place.

Helen's Bridge is an arched stone bridge embellished in moss that leads the way to Zealandia, an incredible Tudor-style mansion. John Brown, grandson of one of the founding families of western North Carolina, envisioned the estate and began construction before heading west during the gold rush. He abandoned the project in search of wealth in California, only to be disappointed. His desires led him to New Zealand next. But the dream never left his heart. He returned to North Carolina to finish what he started and completed Zealandia on Beaucatcher Mountain in 1889. Unfortunately, Brown did not get to enjoy his dreamland home for very long; he passed away in 1895.

Zealandia was then acquired in 1904 by Philip Henry of Australia, who was hoping to begin anew after the loss of his beloved wife. He was inspired by the bustling new city of Asheville, which was rumored to be an "elegant resort community" of its time. Henry quickly made an impression on the city by becoming involved in the local arts and building the city's first art museum. His passion for the arts could be witnessed throughout the manor with displays of Remington paintings, historic armor, curios from around the world, and a lamp from Pompeii, just to mention a few recorded prized possessions. He opened his home to the public so that other art appreciators could relish his collection.

Henry also had a profound appreciation for horses. Seeking to transform his already sizable residence into a more fitting abode, Henry expanded the estate by making personal improvements. For his pride in equestrian pursuits, a Tudor-style horse stable was part of that expansion. I imagine Mr. Henry took part in societal outings such as the Kentucky Derby, which began in the 19th century, based on the recordings of his interests. With the Kentucky state line nearby, attendees from all over the Appalachian region and the Deep South would flock to the event, dressing to the nines and eagerly bidding their highest dollars on their favored contestants. Although Mr. Henry was not a professional horse trainer, his admiration for these graceful animals was evident in his decision to house them within the grand stables for the occasional ride through the mountain trails.

Very little is ever recorded about the workers of manors and wealthy families. All we have are rumors and stories to help us fill in the blanks when it comes to discovering the working class of this time. On the occasions that records are found, they offer very little detailed information about their lives. The same goes for discovering who Helen was in this case. There was hardly anything on paper other than the oral tradition passed on of her sad story. When I close my eyes and imagine who she may have been, I envision a woman with tough skin but a tender heart.

In this painted portrayal, I imagine that Helen is accustomed to tending to the home by performing numerous household duties at a young age. In the mornings before school, as the Sun gently rose over the hills, she'd slip on her shoes and head out to the chicken coop for breakfast eggs, helping prepare the meal for her younger siblings beside her mother. After school, she'd change into attire specifically for chores to keep the laundry minimal. The list of afternoon tasks would vary depending on what her parents had already accomplished. In preparation for dinner, she'd assist her mother in making dinner biscuits, combining flour, freshly churned butter, and milk from the family cow, with a touch of buttermilk. She'd shape each piece of dough and place the pan in the oven. Once golden brown, they'd be served with a drizzle of honey for a sweet treat.

When she got older, she had a daughter. Though her daughter's name remains unrecorded, I'm certain it was a fine one. Helen probably saw the opportunity at Zealandia as a chance for a better future for her little family. Rumors had it that both she and her young daughter were employed there, perhaps as a way to support their household. I imagine their daily horse ride to work, crossing the arched stone bridge on a crisp autumn morning, the oak leaves a captivating apple red, like the ones they snacked on during the ride there. The fog would linger as they rode, slowly dissipating as the day wore on.

Their route offered a view of Asheville's flourishing cityscape before they passed through the towering iron gates of Zealandia. Helen might have wondered why such a small family needed over sixty bedrooms. Growing up in a family where space was limited, she couldn't help but ponder the need for excessiveness. Yet, she held no judgment in her heart. A devout woman, she believed in the dangers of harboring bitter thoughts. She cautiously approached her work, aware of the life-changing opportunities it could bring for her and her daughter, making the long hours worthwhile.

That is, until one dreadful day. Stories claim that Helen was cleaning inside the manor, while her daughter was working out at the stables. The historical records and town lore are vague about how the fire occurred, saying only that it was detrimental to the entire stable extension. Mr. Henry's equestrian heart broke at the loss of horses and glorious construction. But Mr. Henry's heartbreak couldn't have been anywhere near the heartbreak of dear Helen.

When Helen heard of the fire, she quickly ran outdoors for her daughter, only to find that it was too late. The roaring flames had already taken her little soul. The weeping of a mourning mother is unimaginable. The tough skin that had gotten Helen through all her youth shattered. There was nothing worth living for without her other half. As she grieved the loss of her sweet daughter, she crossed the bridge on her way home and found herself in such deep sadness that she took her own life there. Her sorrow is buried in the stones.

The fire must have been a mirror to the future of Zealandia, as the estate became a shadow of Beaucatcher Mountain. It wasn't long before the building's architecture slowly eroded. After the interstate expansion into Asheville, a portion of the estate, including the public art museum, was damaged. It continued to be passed down to other wealthy family members who would later decide to downsize the home. Eventually, it would be sold to another family, only for no one to really make it home again. The property remains closed and off-limits for public visitations. There are no future plans for the estate. It sits there as a ghost with a haunted past.

But Helen's spirit will never forget the tragedy of this place. Her presence is known by locals who feel the need to prove her ghostly existence. Curious minds drive on the street where Helen's Bridge is accessible off Windswept Drive. Mindfulness is always appreciated when approaching the dead, but the stories I've been told demonstrate that it isn't a universal practice. The ghost of Helen appears when she is searching for her daughter's remains. She wanders back and forth on the bridge, visiting the old grounds of the tragic scene, only to return once again without her. Time repeats itself, and she looks once again another night. Nothing. Those who are keen on finding out whether the ghost of Helen is true drive underneath the bridge to call out her name three times. The description of her ghost is much like any other in that her presence is a white glow. Other times nothing happens, and visitors leave disappointed. Meanwhile, some claim that their vehicle has difficulty restarting, as if the battery had been completely drained.

Despite the truth of Helen and her story, the bridge acts as an anchor to a soul of the past. If curiosity strikes, I'd encourage you to tread lightly. Respect goes a long way with the living, and the dead are no different.

Runion and Laurel River Trail: Madison County, North Carolina

This local ghost story was shared with me by Trisha Moser of Madison County. It has been edited for clarity.

> So I live in Madison County close to Mars Hill, towards Hot Springs. There's Laurel River right there and there's a trail that runs along the river that's really flat. That used to be Runion. It's like a ghost town. . . . Runion used to be a little sawmill town and so there are train tracks near there. The trail along the river is super flat because I think that's where the tracks originated, but there was a sawmill village in the late like 1800s to about 1925. It's great to hike in the winter because all the leaves are off the trees and you can actually access Runion—in the summer there's always snakes out there. It's so overgrown you can't see anything.
>
> In February 2011 we hiked up to Runion and found a solid concrete structure. It may have been a trestle of some sort for the train. It was three really solid walls, and there were some foundations of old houses. There's still one standing. I haven't been up there in the winter since then, but there was a big chimney still standing. We also found a concrete flagpole foundation. . . . We figured it was

because it was this round concrete on the ground with a hole in it. It said, "WNC let freedom ring 1917" on it. It was super cool.

Later that summer my husband and I went out there and camped right along the river. There was a great swimming hole. We had two dogs at the time, and we went out there and we're like, we'll just pack in and swim and hang out and camp. Everything was cool. You know, no issues, no heebie-jeebies.

And then it starts getting dark. My husband had camped out there before, and I felt fine being out there. Then once it got dark, the dogs stuck a little closer. And then when we went to bed, we both just laid there, and it was one of those things, like, "Are you still awake?" "Yeah. Are you awake?" The dogs never laid their heads down. They sat by the door of the tent with their heads up, really paying attention all night long.

As the night went on and we were trying to sleep, we heard something like metal on metal. If you've ever listened to a train move, like kind of pulling in somewhere—not chugging down tracks, but moving—it sometimes makes this really awful screeching sound. We both were like, "Did you hear that?" It was just out of nowhere, this like metal-on-metal noise.

Later, we heard a baby crying. There's no one else camping out there. I mean, there's no one around. It wasn't a bobcat, it wasn't a coyote, it wasn't our dogs, it was like a baby crying. We were both like, "Holy cow, did you hear that?" We're all the way down this trail. We're not going to pack up at, you know, three in the morning and hike out of there. We want to be safe in our tent. We're like, "In the morning, we're hiking out of here." Then when the Sun came, we were packing up.

After doing some of my own digging, I found that local author Jan C. Plemmons had written a book on the Runion ghost town, *A Visit to Runion: A Ghost Town of Western North Carolina*. Her father had been born in the sawmill town, and she was able to uncover its rich history.

Lingering spirits are common in these abandoned towns scattered throughout the region. Although the towns themselves lie dormant, they have witnessed the births and deaths of many generations. Trisha pointed out that remnants of homes built for sawmill workers still stood on the trail. I imagine that this is a physical representation of the souls who once called these woods home and why they may still linger.

Gifts from the Woods: Haywood County, North Carolina

Before diving into this specific series of stories, I want to provide some context on who this generous, soulful human is. This series of events was shared with me by a dear friend and mentor from the mountains, Shannon Bear of Haywood County.

When we met, I recognized her spirit and felt immediately that I was in good hands. The connection and depth of her relationship to these mountains are unlike anything I have ever witnessed. She's knowledgeable in the sense that she packs every necessity one could imagine for a hike in the woods. Always in preparation for the unlikely chance of getting lost. Her hair is vibrant like the fire in cauldrons and her laugh is contagious like a roar. She curses like a sailor but with a smile on her face because it ain't anything but a bit of teasing. Some of my most profound moments in these woods have been in her ushered guidance. There are no words that can capture this woman's soul. Just spend time with her, and then you'll get it.

I disclose a bit of our personal connection for a few reasons: one, when Shannon shares with me something that happened during her recent outing in the Blue Ridge Mountains, she ain't fibbing; and two, there's no question that Shannon has a thoughtful and respectful approach to spirits from all realms here. With her presence, I have witnessed such unearthly confrontations in these wooded meeting grounds. Our time together has included receiving blessings from the spirits, as much as it was them relaying that we may be overstaying our welcome.

The sequence of events that follows her story illustrates the various spirits present here. My objective is to capture tales that reflect the essence of this region, no matter how peculiar they may seem to ordinary people. Shannon is a treasure trove of such stories. I am deeply grateful and honored to have this practitioner in my life, and I appreciate the opportunity to share her experiences with y'all. Here is an edited transcript of some of her stories:

[A few years ago,] I was in the woods to do an alchemy session with a client. Any time I go to a camping spot—now, this is just like a general tip for anybody in the woods to learn from, you know, good old Carl, the original mountain man! But you check the firepit always. You need to be aware of your surroundings anyway, but especially if you're going into a place where people have camped. You might find a pocketknife, for Christ's sake. You might find extra rope or something that could be potentially good for you in a camping setting or survival setting. This is ingrained into me—you check the space and especially the firepit. It's because people just lose shit all the time. I've found ferro rods, pocketknives, ball caps, all kinds of cool shit.

So, first things first, we inspect the firepit. (You've seen this firsthand.) My client and I get to the spot, and you know how I am, I show everyone the area. First, I encourage my clients to tell me what calls to you, what feels good, what's hollering at you, why—you know, let's lean into it and let's do the work.

So my client is like, "This looks great, I love this, and I'm really drawn to the river." I set my shit down, try to move it out of the way of photographs. My bag is way off to the side and she sets her little bags down too. I had asked her if she brought an offering because, you know, gotta have an offering. Well, she brought some lavender. You know me, I have my tobacco offering for the very end. So my bag is probably, let's say, twenty yards off to the side out of the way.

And we get started. I've checked the site. Everything looks good. No glass, no yuck, no nothin'. Just pristine. I create the circle and the session starts.

We're mostly through the alchemy session. The fire's going nicely. We go down to the river—doing our thing. It's so good. My client feels so grounded and cleansed. So we get back to the firepit and she says, "I think I want to get my lavender." And I'm like, "That's a great idea." This is the perfect transition in our ritual. I look down at the rocks, and what do I see? A little pile of tobacco. I kid you not. Now, that was not there when we got started.

My client looks at me and I look at her, and we kind of have this moment of, What? She didn't bring tobacco. Well, mine's twenty yards away in my pack, you know, like I have not taken out that thing yet! We're not ready to close this ceremony yet. I'm not ready to make this offering. I have no idea how to look at that. I don't know how it got there.

Now, in this same area down the trail, there was a time when I was in deep grief. I'm not doing well. There's a lot of stuff going on. My dad just died, and I needed to return to myself. I needed a debrief with Mama, anyway, right? I needed to pour this out of my chest.

I wanted to take my heart out and just like set it in the river. You know that feeling of just sadness and grief and the weight and all of it.

So, same thing. I come in; I check the firepit. Then, I'm at a birch tree. This is a very special spot. The last time that I was in the woods with Dad was at this spot. Nothing's at that firepit, everything's fine. My friend and I go our separate ways for a moment. I'm foraging mushrooms. We come back and I'm thinking, I really want to set up an altar. This feels good to me.

I'm literally sitting on a rock and building this altar, in a way for heart healing and for grief, to just like channel through. I put my hand down, and what else is sitting on this rock? It's a 40 Smith and Wesson. This was one of Dad's favorite calibers. It's been there for . . . I don't even know how long. It's jam-packed with dirt. It could have fallen out of his pack one time when we were out there. I do not have a clue how it ended up in my spot at the firepit. I had already gotten the fire going, had already explored everything. There was no showcasing sitting there before. And there it was, just as I'm starting to build my altar.

In this next story, I'm with the same client as before. Instead of down the trail, we're now at the same spot with my friend rather than near the river. We're there to do some mother work. Needed to relief some grief.

So, again, I check the spot. I'm in the exact same spot as the original story with the tobacco. I'm building the fire from that place. There's nothing there, everything's fine. The only thing that was different this time was this big birch log that was sitting off to the side, which someone probably intended for firewood. My client is doing a meditation. She's deep, deep in it and I think, I need to get the fire going. I'm getting the fire going in the same spot as before.

And to my right, next to the birch tree, I keep feeling this sensation like something wants to be noticed. Almost like someone was saying, "I'm right here, please, you have to see me." I look over at the birch log, and guess what? An herb bundle with garden sage is just lying there. When we got there, there was nothing there. I swear to God. Same area. I'm like, you can't make this up. I have no clue how that thing got there. I don't know. I don't know the energetic pull that was like, "Notice me, notice me, notice me, notice me." We ended up returning it to the water because we noticed it was a bit damp.

Naturally, I am always intrigued when Shannon speaks about this deep relationship with nature and how she learned of this profound connection being raised in Haywood County.

I have always felt the safest in the natural world. And Dad was a survivalist, you know. Well, he was a mountain man, so survival skills were very important to him. It's not like every time we went out, I was able to commune in the way that felt good to me. There were times where I'd be like, you go do your compass course—I'm going over here. And he respected that. While he was trying to instill skills that would help keep me alive in an emergency, he intended for me to have a deep connection to the woods. He really honored the fact that I wanted to lay down and look at the aura of the trees and feel myself sinking down into the earth in a way that was deeply restorative, no matter what was going on, like with whatever stress was occurring in my life.

You know, understanding how deeply connected we are and how much the earth and non-humankind want to respond and want to be in relationship has been so amazing to watch unfold over the last several years. Since he died, I'm having to understand what my connection with the earth looks like.

I asked her about some of her earliest memories of encountering and communicating with spirits of the land.

When I was four or five, we were in Transylvania County, over near Yellow Gap. We went to what I call the "pine stand," and as I'm walking along I start seeing these little flashes of light out of the corner of my eye, these sparkly little things, and I'm thinking, *What are you?* I'm just trying to figure it out, you know? So I keep going, following my whims, chasing after these wisps. I was just so happy, blissed out, skipping along and following these little sparkles, these lights, just doing my thing. Then I come to this spot where a tree had fallen, so I had the choice to go over the tree or go left. I decided to go left.

I started down the road and came across what seemed like hundreds of fairy rings, though it was probably just twenty or fifty—still, in my memory, it felt like hundreds. It was like fairy rings all over. I had the best time. I went to every single one of them, following those little sparkles wherever they led. I mean, one would lead to the center of a fairy ring and then it would expand, and I'd be like, "Wow, where's the next one!" Dad just leaned against a pine tree keeping eyes on me.

I felt like I was veil hopping for a hundred years, you know? And to this day, I can take you right to those fairy rings. Oh my gosh, I love that they're still there, so much.

The Curious Brown Mountain Lights: Burke County, North Carolina

This is a personal story about one of my hometown's most curious legends. It was a crisp late-summer afternoon when my friend group decided to venture out to witness the well-known Brown Mountain lights near the Linville Gorge of western North Carolina. Before this evening venture, I had never heard of them in my years of growing up in the area. A friend of a friend, who became the guide for the excursion, had told us about it.

He mentioned that the story of these lights was that they were the lost souls of settlers from war who were trying to find their way home with their lanterns. Other tales shared that perhaps they were the lost souls of Indigenous People who resided here before colonization. Then, there were additional rumors that they were lights from extraterrestrials roaming our planet. Religious folks believed it was the miracle work of divinity that these lights rose from the mountain and into the sky, disappearing and reappearing in an inconsistent pattern.

Many attempts had been made to identify these lights due to the nationwide interest in this bizarre occurrence. In 1922, a geologist from the federal government was assigned to discover the source of the odd scenarios occurring on Brown Mountain once and for all. His conclusion was based on "multiple reasonings," such as traffic, household lights, and occasional brush fires. The generations of mountain folks who bore witness to these lights and their exceptional encounters were skeptical of the scientist's conclusion, as perhaps, after years of speculation, it was too simple an answer to such curious events.

We approached a dirt road that led to a hiking trail with a rusted old gate just ahead—an attempt to prevent further intruders from climbing this hilltop. Despite these efforts, it didn't stop delinquent youngsters such as myself and my group of friends. As the Sun dipped, we hiked up the trail to an unofficial lookout that only a local would know of. Perhaps this trail had a specific name. I wouldn't know of it now. It was an unbeaten path from a paved mountain road that was hidden from the outside world.

We continued exchanging stories about the Brown Mountain lights and other menacing local lore on the way up. Flashlights in hand, we hiked for what may have been just over a mile under the dense cascades of trees that watched us as we climbed. Before my thighs completely gave out and the Sun finally went to sleep with the Moon awakening, we approached the top, a flat overlook with a single boulder in the center. The friend of a friend smirked as we sighed with relief and said, "You see here? They say a cult of witches comes up here once a month to do their sacrifices." The others winced at this vision, laughing nervously at each other.

My eyes were fixated just ahead of the hills, waiting ever so impatiently at the thought that maybe we wouldn't get the pleasure of witnessing the infamous Brown Mountain lights. As we'd learned through countless recollections, there was no certainty that they'd appear every night. It was based on the perfect conditions—whatever those were. But lo and behold, shortly after we arrived at the potential witch's spot for rituals, there they were.

Just ahead, we saw orbed lights appear from the mountain. They'd rise up into the air just above the mountain, then disappear. A handful of them at a time. No clouds were in sight that night, so it wasn't like they were hiding. They were twinkling around the low mountain. It was eerie and perplexing. *What could they be?* I remember that for a moment, we became very quiet as we watched them rise and disappear. *What if they were lost* souls? *Was there any way to help them home? Will they always be here on this mountain, roaming till the end of time?* Countless thoughts raced in my mind as we were silent. The darkness of the night felt dense, and a feeling overcame us that perhaps we were not the only ones present. My friend suggested it was probably time for us to get back home. The others agreed, and we pointed our flashlights down the hill while the trees watched us depart.

LORE OF THE LITTLE PEOPLE

The trail ahead of me is steep, but I'm too enthralled by the green hues glistening in the midsummer Sun to notice. The rays press hard against my porcelain, freckled skin. My body hot and sticky from the humid air. A voice ahead of me calls for my attention. "You see that?" My aunt's arm extends to the side of the trail, pointing to where a tree trunk meets the soil. "There's a heart shape made from the moss on that tree trunk. It's a reminder that we're loved, and we're not alone." She smiles and continues on the path.

At that moment, the world around me was ignited with a new kind of life from my aunt's stories. My eyes had been opened to this idea that we're always walking alongside unseen spirits. Everything was breathing with me. Their lungs filled with the same mountain air I longed to enjoy forever. My feet treaded along the trail ahead. My body weight heavy as it craved refreshment at the waterfall near the end. The ferns beside me waved as I walked by. Moss hugged the boulders piercing through the ground. "Now, keep your eyes peeled to find any other heart shapes in nature," she called back. My eyes began to observe every tree branch, every stump, every rock, every flower, every stone all the way to the end and back.

We settled on a rock for my aunt to pull out her sketchbook and she began drawing the scenic wooded view ahead. The trees in community with one another. Exchanging their chatter with every gust of wind, their branches waving back and forth. A sound so elegant and freeing that you can't help but close your eyes and be lifted to the sky. Looking down at yourself, a serene state of mind. A peek of flora shows through the long grass, the delicate white blossoms spread across the landscape. A collection of branches had fallen and created a natural archway in the distance—a scene fit for a mythical creature's home.

Her voice interrupted my daydream again. "You see over there?" she says, nodding toward the archway. I confirm with a soft, "Yeah."

"Well, I'm sure that's where some faeries live. You can tell because there's a natural ring formation on the ground with mushrooms from their songs. They may be nearby. Keep your eyes peeled."

Nothing in my young body wanted to move. I desperately wanted to see these little creatures. The ones I read all about before bedtime. The ones I thought lived in my backyard creek. The ones that were featured on the wallpaper my mother had plastered all over my sister's themed nursery. They wore flowers for dresses and made crowns with the blossoms. My favorite was the buttercup.

This was only the beginning of my fascination with faeries, these mysterious nature spirits. I was told the kid-friendly version of who they were, inspired by the Victoria era. They frolicked in enchanted wooded fields and took care of nature around them. Their stories were lively and playful. They tended to the bees to ensure they found pollen. They played with toads in the pond and sat on lily pads. They'd gather in gardens, sit on mushrooms, enjoy fruits, and play flutes. They were delightful creatures. I wanted to be just like them, surrounded by the beauty of nature, wearing my favorite flower as a dress—either a sunflower or an iris.

As I've grown older and dived deeper into the origins of faery lore, I've recognized that quite a bit of information misled my young heart. They are not entirely of this earthly world. They have one foot in our physical realm and the other in the spiritual realm. A life that travels in the in-between.

Belief in these entities spans across the world, appearing in plenty of tales. It is entirely impossible to dive into each culturally specific definition of faeries in just one book, but there are a few notable tales that have formed our perceptions here in the southern hills.

The belief in these spirits is so widespread that it is hard to know for sure whether one story is truer than another. I believe the stories we hear about these spirits in Appalachia from the Indigenous People are the most sincere, and the best way to understand their nature regionally. These spirits of this mountain range often go by the name Little People, which is the English translation of the Cherokee name Yunwi Tsundi. You'll hear locals call them other names too, like good folk, drawing from the Scottish and Irish folktales and impressions. Here, they have taken on a unique persona, birthed from Cherokee folktales and blended with the British Isles diaspora's associations with such spirits. This shared perception mentions these spirits live close to the land, with only a few capable of seeing them with their naked eye. You'll hear nuanced tones of their presence. Either a practitioner finds that they're a helpful hand, while others acknowledge their existence, and that's about it. Just like how we approach other spirits—saints, deities, angels, etc.—they are no different. It would be rather silly to describe what to expect, as each is rather individual in personality, and the result depends entirely on the practitioner's approach and intention.

In this region, this nature spirit's reputation is most known to help carry out petitioned requests, while others may be rather skeptical and avoid contact. A practitioner may establish a reciprocal relationship with offerings, acknowledging their unseen neighbors, in hopes that they become guardians of their gardens and household, or help carry out petitions and healing work. Without encountering the Little People yourself, there is no certainty of the outcome. It is best practice to approach with caution and the best of intentions.

They can be found inhabiting landmarks that represent the liminal, such as riversides, caves, and among the trees. Where I currently call home is surrounded by hawthorn trees, three of which are across the street from the window I'm looking out now. I like to think of them as the Three Sisters. I've witnessed three seasonal cycles with them now, and it's clear that they're guardians of our small community. They've fostered a few of our local robin families. As I walk in the early hours, I'll be sure to pay them a visit. In the warm summer days, the aroma of their blossoms is enticing. But I know better than to indulge. Instead, I forage some flowers after an offering of eggshells at the base of the trunk to be used in a salve for heart healing.

During my morning briefings, I'd feel a lingering eye while talking among the Three Sisters. The sensation of stares was stronger in the evening. I've learned it's best not to dawdle too long when the Sun goes down between the Three Sisters. I followed suit with the stories I had read and what others had shared about making offerings of sweet breads, which seemed to please these nature spirits, as the unsettled feelings of staring began to subside, though they didn't completely disappear. Perhaps we are not meant to be friends, but we can remain cordial as I consult the Three Sisters.

Recently, I've seen an unfamiliar silver stray cat linger around the neighborhood. It tries to be sneaky in the early morning hours and closely watches as I walk. I've heard tales about these spirits taking the form of animals. Cats were included in the list, especially in the color white. This silver cat has piercing green eyes, and I am almost certain it is not of this physical world.

SUPERSTITIONS
OF SOUTHERN APPALACHIA

The Sun begins its descent behind the rugged mountain ridge across the way. As the blue hour approaches, stars twinkle above me, and the crickets orchestrate their summer song. The shadows begin to cast on the hillside as I sit observing from the trunk of my car. As I start packing up my picnic dinner to head home, something catches the corner of my eye. Against the misted dusk, a petite crimson figure effortlessly glides and perches atop the cove's signage—a cardinal. A familiar friend that tugs at my heart. Cardinals are said to bring messages from the otherworld, representing past loved ones from the spirit realm. Having just lost two significant people in my life just a year apart, this encounter with grief and death resonates deeply. The cardinal glances my way for a fleeting moment before soaring off, summoned to its next visitation.

Appalachians are familiar with such signs. The region harbors numerous superstitions and omens that were birthed from the long history of hardship where death trailed close behind. The craggy terrain, a natural barrier to the outside world, seems to retain rather than forget old wives' tales. The region's complex history provides fertile ground for such skeptical beliefs to bloom. Footprints of the many lives lived and lost are imprinted forever in the soil. It carries both life and death. A nourishment for our gardens and yet a blanket for our past loved ones buried beneath. A place where assumptions of natural patterns conclude life's greatest mysteries and mishaps.

In the depths of the coal mines, where darkness hung like a heavy shroud and the steady rhythm of picks striking the mountainside echoed through the valley, life proceeded in a fragile balance. Caution permeated every aspect of their existence, a daily acceptance of the risks they faced. With the lack of care about working conditions from these extraction companies, families at home understood that not everyone might return safely. Believing in the unnatural felt most natural for a people who faced immense darkness. The miners from Britain, including Cornish and Welsh, brought with them mining superstitions from their homelands. Running late to work was thought to be bad luck, as well as encountering a rabbit or black cat crossing their path on the way to the mines. They'd turn around and go back home for the day. Dreams also played a role in determining the miner's fate. If a dream featured broken shoes or an accident involving the miner, then it would be recommended that they also stay home.

Farmers also relied heavily on nature's signs for a bountiful harvest and successful season. Weather patterns and nature delivered signs and omens that prepared the farmers either way. They'd be able to figure out whether the upcoming winter season would be short and sweet or long and brutal. Other signs foretold that spring would arrive earlier than expected, a breath of fresh air. Nature foreshadowed what the farmer could expect in hopes of implementing solutions to ensure their crops were safe and sound.

Omens may have been born from an era of great uncertainty, but they acted as answers to the unexplainable. The cardinal that visited me in a time of grief was a reminder that all is not forgotten. That the spirits of those whom I personally lost were present with me at that moment. The cardinal continues to be that sign of comfort for others who share similar grief. Superstitions and omens were birthed for this reason. They gave shape to the unfamiliar and unknown, providing some some semblance of understanding amidst despair. With no concrete answers for why things happen, humans decided to look to nature to find meaning and answers. Omens, whether good or bad, provided an explanation of things that could not easily be comprehended. They'd look to patterns or coincidences to make sense of it all. Perhaps you've experienced a stream of bad luck. One day, you stub your toe. The next, you break your favorite mug. On the third day, your car breaks down. Each passing day is progressively worse. Then, you recall that you had broken a small compact mirror on your last trip. The pieces then fall into place, and the superstition takes form that the broken mirror delivered such bad luck.

With superstitions and omens, the blend of the mystical and mundane intertwined, resulting in the region's folk magic. There was no point in risking hardship if there was a way to prevent it. When resources were minimal and solutions were hidden, people would turn to these ways even if some were not fully "proven." Growing up, I was told to hold my breath as we drove by cemeteries unless I wanted to carry home a ghost. Did I whole-heartedly believe that would be the case? Not entirely. But I didn't want to run the risk and so I have embedded that practice into my life. It's more of a precaution than anything else.

Of Life and Death

Before kids were the appropriate age to have the birds and the bees talk, whimsical tales were used to explain how babies came to be. Most famously, babies were delivered by a bird, such as the stork. The stork was recorded as the delivery bird in North Carolina. The stork may have been designated with such an honor, but other animals played similar roles. Some versions say a mother raccoon discovers the baby in the woods and delivers them to their mother. Others say babies were found in mysterious places like tree stumps and sugar barrels. Meanwhile, recorded over in Kentucky, the child came down from an apple tree to sit on their family's roof for eight weeks until the doctor found them to deliver to the mother. For this reason, birds like the stork represent fertility and new beginnings. Apples are also known to be associated with fertility, blessings, love, and protection.

When it came time for childbirth, there were a few things a healer or granny would do to diminish the emotional and physical pain. Aside from preparing tea blends and hot, wet towels, and gathering the emotional support of neighboring caretakers, various fumigation blends were made to burn underneath the mother's bed. Storing items underneath the bed to aid the mother in birth seemed to be a recurring practice. Not only did burning hair or chicken feathers ensure a smooth birth, but so did placing items such as an open Bible with intertwined hazel twigs in the form of a cross. This Kentucky charm was also stored underneath the woman's pillow. Sharp items like an opened pair of scissors or an ax were also positioned under the bed to help cut the pain in half. Steel is long associated with preventing any bewitchment that could cause sickness. It's affirmed here in the practice of a smooth childbirth that it was also used to protect the mother's health. Opened scissors were not only used to cut pain in half, but also the formation of a cross deters any malevolent spirits and witches away from the bed.

Other superstitions relay that the mother should avoid partaking in certain activities and events to protect her unborn child from bearing marks or adopting mirrored behavior. Mothers were discouraged from attending funerals to avoid a fragile, ghostly child. The same goes for visiting gravesites. Anything related to conversing with the dead was discouraged. It was also believed that similar behaviors of the mother would be passed on to the child. My mother always told me the reason I'm a sensitive soul is because she watched her favorite soap opera while giving birth to me. Certain days would also gift the child specific features or abilities that are recited in nursery rhymes; no doubt, we've all heard the rhyme that starts *"Wednesday's child is full of woe, Thursday's child has far to go . . ."*. Recorded in Kentucky, a child born on Christmas Day was given the gift of understanding the language of animals.

There were some predictions that could help determine the baby's sex, too. I've heard about using a ring at the end of a piece of thread, or simply a necklace, as a pendulum just above the pregnant belly. The direction of the pendulum determined the baby's sex, such as swinging back and forth if it's a boy or in a circle if it's a girl. I'm not entirely sure of the accuracy of the practice. (I do wonder, though, if my mother had had this divination performed before my birth if the surprise of me being a girl wouldn't have been so alarming. They were prepared to come home with another boy. But nope! Instead, I was the first granddaughter on my father's side.)

In addition to childbearing, folklore surrounding life's transitions frequently intertwines with beliefs surrounding death. Appalachia is home to some of the most extensive death omens and superstitions. Here, folks have long held intricate beliefs and omens concerning the life cycle, reflecting a deep fear and respect for the inevitable.

In a region that experienced the early death of loved ones working in tough conditions and with unknown illnesses, almost any rarity or unusual natural pattern was recorded as a doom omen. For example, signs were delivered by the simplest of things, such as bread. Should there be a crack on the top of the loaf, it was said that death will soon follow someone in the family. This may seem senseless to us now, but when life delivers empty promises, the only way to grieve is to come up with explanations. Other times, the delivery came in the form of an animal. A long list of animals related to such assumptions was collected in Kentucky. An unfamiliar black cat that was found on the front porch of someone's home would deliver a message that someone would soon die. A crow perched on the home had a similar association with being a messenger of someone's death. Recorded in Tennessee, a black hen coming into the home was an omen to an impending family death.

Other unusual occurrences were deemed warnings that death was lingering in every corner. Sometimes the omen would come in the form of burning of the ear, otherwise known as "death's bells." Today, we assume that this is a clue that someone is speaking ill of us, or that a spirit is trying to convey a message. But early folks had no understanding of why they would randomly hear the ringing. It was almost as if Death itself were ringing the church bell to inform them that someone would be taken. In Kentucky, which ear the ringing occurred in would determine the direction of where the death would be heard from, such as the east or west.

As someone who is familiar with death, I have found that the relationship is much like knowing a neighbor but not necessarily being interested in hosting them. Instead, it's an acknowledgment of nature's cycle of life. An understanding that death is always present. I don't mean to come across as solemn. My grievances have led me to this mindset of acceptance. Death can be physical as much as it is spiritual. This leads to transmutation, the taking of something to transform it into something else entirely, the way our own soil teaches us that after every winter, new seeds bloom from the previous generations. For something to come alive, something else must die. Appalachians have a profound understanding of this.

Of Land and Sky

Nature's cycles and patterns served as a communicator for the Appalachian farmer and homesteader, anticipating what lies ahead. In a deep trance, connecting with my own farming ancestors, I often hear to "look to the heavens" and pay attention to nature around me as a guiding source for answers. We can be given direction by observing weather patterns and cycles as foresight of what's to come. Such insights reflect the lore that many farmers and naturalists are familiar with. Is there a harsh winter ahead? An early spring? Nature will show us the signs.

You may already be familiar with weather lore that speaks on predictions, such as "April showers bring May flowers." This has become a universal superstition that many recite today. Have you monitored your own flower beds to see if April showers did, in fact, bring about the May flowers? Other signs sent from the sky were monitored by farmers and sailors at bay. Sailors relied heavily on the sky to be their compass with the stars as well as the painted sunsets and sunrises. "Red at night, a sailor's delight. Red in the morning, a sailor's warning." The red in the morning would indicate foul weather ahead. A similar expression is found in the mountains of Kentucky with the phrase "circle around the moon, rain soon; circle around the sun, rain none." I don't recommend staring directly at the Sun to determine whether a circle is around it or not, so perhaps glancing up at the night sky to reference the Moon for the upcoming forecast is best. A circle around the Moon also suggests that an unsettling event is on the horizon and precautions should be taken.

Naturally, I am an early bird, always waking up at the slightest sign of sunlight peeking through the blinds. As soon as it does, I slip on my shoes and leash up the dog for a morning stroll. During these early mornings, I will take note of nature around. The mourning doves call and the smell of the heat rises from the asphalt sidewalk with honeysuckle bushes nearby. Some mornings, the views are clear; other times, there's a fog lingering below the hills. Before knowing any superstition about early morning fog being a sign of clear weather ahead, I noticed that the day shifted into clear blue skies and warmer temperatures.

The sky may hint at what lies ahead, but animals and the land also offer guidance of one's fate. In my practice, I've taken notice of certain animals that come to send divine messages. A slug that is moving slowly on the pavement on my evening walk is a sign that maybe now is a good time to take things slow. Enjoy life's little moments without the need to rush. This can be hard to incorporate every day, so sometimes a slug reminder is helpful. Other times, a crow will caw nearby, and even though they've got a reputation for being a sign of death or unwanted visitors, I also see them as a sign to face what it is that I'm holding on to that could be a personal barrier. The death of an old habit may be required. As I sit in the backyard, rummaging through the grass and inspecting every clover, coming across a four-leaf clover enhances my chances of receiving good luck in a situation. I'll enclose it in my palm and make a wish, then store it in a jar for my curio cabinet as a good luck charm.

In the corner of my room, a spider begins its web. They're helpful when retrieving lost items with the spoken charm: "Spitter, spitter spider, tell me where the [insert your lost item here] is, and I'll give you a drink of cider." I've recognized the presence of spiders very frequently. Ever since I was young, I could "hear" the spider in the room and could always locate it. Funny, isn't that? Even though they are meant to help me find things, it is I who am always the one finding them when nobody else notices. I used to joke that it was because of our family name Webb. That justification may have been a bit juvenile, but I still chuckle as an adult because my relationship with spiders has not changed. Instead, it reminds me of the power of weaving webs of creativity to capture fleeting muses.

Of Home and Hearth

The home acts as a medium for communication of signs and countering omens. It serves not only as a sanctuary from the outside world but also as a focal point for superstitions. When observing folk beliefs, any mishaps or unexplainable events are often looked at with a raised eyebrow, followed quickly by preventative measures. The practice of discernment should be applied when peculiar happenings occur. A personal rule of mine that I'd like to propose is to pay close attention to unusual activity occurring three times.

Specific spaces within the home are liminal, such as doorways, chimneys, and mirrors. When standing in a doorway, one can feel the threshold's liminality, neither fully inside nor outside. Old Appalachian burial customs are a testament to domestic perspectives of the threshold. Prior to funeral homes and caretaking facilities, folks passed away in the comfort of their home with family by their side and would remain in the home for a few days. A few practices to ensure their spirit crossed over safely were taken into account. Mirrors would be covered with a blanket, and the windows would be opened to release the spirit from the home. After the neighbors assigned to make the casket finished, they would help move the body to the graveside. They'd ensure that the body was carried through the doorway of the house feet first. Otherwise, the spirit would remain tied to the home.

Careful consideration was also given to the objects brought into the home. It was discouraged to bring in any sort of tools used for labor, such as axes, saws, or gardening tools. The working tool held the energy from the worker's day, and bringing it inside meant also bringing inside work stresses. If someone inadvertently brought such tools inside, they would reverse their steps slowly out of the door to expel the potential bad luck.

Another critical aspect determining the household's fate was done with a pair of shoes. Shoes belonging to a deceased coal miner were often placed on the table. Therefore, it was considered unlucky for anyone living in the house to leave their shoes on the table, as it was believed to bring misfortune upon them. Shoes also were capable of overturning bad luck or warning against an untimely passing. This derives from the shared regional belief that items belonging to someone are a tether to their fate and energy. Old working shoes in particular contained the individual's essence, making them a precious item. Shoes have been stored in thresholds like chimneys and doorways across European historic recordings, to be used as wards against witches and spirits. The shoes held superstitious associations in the Appalachian region, with folks utilizing them for magical work. The simple act of turning a shoe upside down meant to override a bad omen of unexpected misfortune. The same goes for placing items within the shoes, such as coins, in hopes of protecting the wearer from mishaps or bewitchment. They were also positioned in doorways and hearths as a protection charm from those with ill intentions who might enter the home. My father used to have a pair of handmade wooden clogs with his name carved on the side, gifted to him by another family member he never named. They were always stored beside the fireplace.

Ensuring the home was clean also avoided the possibility of a bad omen. Preventative measures were taken to establish the home's protective barrier from the outside. I'm sure you've heard of throwing salt over your left shoulder to prevent bad luck. It was believed that creating salt lines prevents unwanted energies from crossing over thresholds too. Other items, such as coins, were stored in windowsills to protect and attract wealth for the household. Cleaning tools such as brooms and dusters, with their association with witches and spirits, were stored near doorways to help sweep away spirits. And lastly, should you accidentally drop a cloth while cleaning, step over it while making a wish before picking it up!

7

THE FINISHED BINDING

The faces of my ancestors have been weathered by time in the photos I've recovered. Some of the family portraits have distant cousins grouped together, standing side by side from eldest to youngest. The tall corn crops tower behind them at their Kentucky homestead. I imagine they'd probably play hide and seek with one another in those fields, carefully making sure no one got lost. A portrait of Great-Grandmother Aggie shows her on a rocking chair on the front porch of her home in Pike County, hands gently placed on her lap with eyes gazing into the camera. Young Mamaw Nora is on one side, with Uncle Denver in his war uniform on the other. Another image shows Great-Great-Grandfather John, with a man I assume is his father, on their porch in Athens County, Ohio, dressed in their Sunday best. The only day they'd catch a break from working the mines. In another, Papaw Webb, at the young age of eighteen, poses in what I imagine to be his car, wearing a white, collared shirt and dark hair slicked back. I see my father's face in his, and recognize the features I've inherited from them both, like our cheekbones and nose. At this age, he was working the mines for about forty-six hours a week with his father. I imagine they'd all have a lot to share with me if I were to be sitting with them in these photos.

Instead, I am sitting around a bonfire with the evening Moon, accompanied by a few folks. The smoke follows me whenever I nudge my camping chair over another inch. "Smoke follows beauty," a husky voice remarks. I've heard this saying a lot and wonder if smoke would nod in agreement. I've always found that it's just a coincidence where the wind is blowing at that exact moment. It never makes it less inconvenient when the smoke makes your eyes water, though.

I have a firm grip on a mason jar filled with clear liquid that reeks of nail polish and apples. Homemade from a gentleman who introduced himself as Uncle Gary upon his arrival. Though, he wasn't my uncle. Around here, people would refer to elders as "uncles" or "aunts" as signs of endearment. It was respectful to refer to a family friend as such. In most cases, they were just as good as blood relatives and sometimes even better. I've got quite a few uncles and aunts that aren't by blood.

It was my first taste of moonshine that night. I made up the story in my mind that it was called that because it was enchanted by the Moon's magical powers of lifting you high into the sky. I wasn't too far off. The liquid would burn as it went down, warming my blood on the crisp autumn night. As if the fire wouldn't do the trick already. The rule was that you'd take your sip and then pass it to the person on your right around the circle. There was no concern about sharing the same mason jar or anything like that back then. Only the single mason jar was left of the ungodly liquid for all to share anyway. Uncle Gary required everyone to give his latest recipe a try.

Stories were exchanged about people I had never heard of. I'd listen anyway. Those who had passed were being revived at this very moment by having their names mentioned. Laughter followed with a knee slap as childhood memories played out. I sat back in my chair, keeping an eye on the moonshine to see how much was left while the folks around me bantered. My heart was full by the swirling of old tales around me. This is how it's all done, isn't it? This is how we catch glimpses of ancestors we may never meet. They live on in our memories and hearts so long as we hold space for them. It's not always done on the night of a bonfire, with apple pie moonshine being passed around. Sometimes it's during a car ride to the airport. Or while visiting a sick one in the hospital. It really doesn't matter where the stories are being told, so long as they are.

Grief tapped my shoulder. I had never shared these kinds of moments with my own family before. It had been years since we'd gathered at the family cabin. I was under the assumption that reunions were a thing of the past. The folks around me are not blood related, but they feel like it. They'd include me in the stories as if I knew all the cousins and grandparents from "up north." I'd chuckle to pretend to be part of the inside jokes.

This exact feeling of belonging is why walking an ancestral path made sense. I may not have heard their magical stories or how they combat against witches, but growing up here gives me enough reason to think they had similar practices without putting a name to it. It's a way for me to discover pieces of myself and place them together by listening and learning as their whispers guide my work.

For some in this region who were taught by their elders, others like me are guided by their spirits and follow the threads left behind. It is not easy. There are some stories that will never be recovered because nobody recognized their value. For that reason, my heart aches from the potential of the rich wisdom left behind in my family tree. It's a bit like navigating a forested labyrinth at night, your hands outstretched in front of you, searching for something to grab hold of and guide you along the path.

Our known and unknown ancestors are the deepest of our roots. They go back generations. And while some names have never been recovered, their presence is surely there. These same ancestors found themselves in these mountains, one way or another, and took matters in their own hands to begin their new lives, never knowing what it would take or the trials they'd endure. Their experiences influenced the folk recordings we've uncovered and the practices of generations who continue to teach the next.

A large apple tree with roots deep beneath the soil experiences new growth every season, with the leftover fruits nourishing the birds and the squirrels. A symbol of familial practices. The roots may be buried, but they are nurtured by many hands. The leaves blossom then fall to their slumber, only to be revived again in the warmer months. The tree bears ripe fruit in early autumn, a gift for lessons learned and a bounty to share with neighbors. The Appalachian tree is deeply rooted and shaped over generations by diverse people drawn from all corners of the world. They are each a branch on this beloved tree. These customs and old ways took root—both literally in the fertile soil and figuratively in every aspect of our lives: our health, our homes, our gardens, our foods, and our magic.

REVOLUTIONIZING TRADITION

By building a foundation for our practice inspired by traditions, we also embrace how times change and bring new twists and turns. Folk magic and witchcraft adapt to meet the needs of the people today. The word "tradition" often leaves a taste in our mouth that there is no room for flexibility, when in fact Appalachia has proven this isn't the case. The region has undergone generations of change, and continues to do so. Some ways are for the better, while others are hell-bent in their ways. The region's religious landscape alone has organically begun shifting away from identifying solely as Christian. It prompts the question of how these magical traditions, once created within this religious framework, will adapt in the hands of those who parted from Christianity and embrace animism or polytheistic practices. If anything, we can learn from those early practitioners and healers who embraced thinking outside the box and doing what needed to be done on their own terms.

It's worth mentioning that while our work is important, it may not wield the change we'd like to see from the entire world. A small act creates a ripple effect, and that is something worth holding on to. The world isn't what our ancestors knew anymore either, and yet some of their traditions offer important lessons that still hold value, like slowing down, being mindful, and being resourceful. These practices applied today can open a path that reconnects us to nature, to our neighbors, and to our resistance, to fight against a system that seeks to overwork and divide us. There's a lot of magic to be experienced in our mountains, if we can just fend off a world that hopes to distance us from it.

You will find ongoing conversations and new written work added to the diverse collection of traditions from this region. The more attention Appalachia receives, the more that is uncovered and embraced. The idea of tradition often means that there is one unified way, but Appalachia shows us that many are celebrated here. You'll see that your neighbors will have different ways of doing things. Just like how some folks may use a pie pan to deflect energy, I'm using it to bake an apple pie offering. But I'll be sure to cut you a slice in hopes that you share what you're doing, understanding that you may not reveal all the tips and tricks, just like I'd keep some to myself. And yet, there will be some shared ground, too. Tradition, when used dangerously, can be a word associated with purity. And there ain't no pure form of folk magic. It is fluid and adaptable, always taking a new form to meet the needs of the practitioner and the people. If you're from this region, taught in this region, and bear roots from this region and approach it all with love and respect, then you're doing it right. Our region's magic is living and breathing. It is not meant to be something of the past, but rather a guide in our work and our unique paths.

Old narratives still need rewriting to better represent what Appalachia is about. This affirms that the work of the Appalachian practitioner has not yet been concluded. While there's been notable progress since the olden days, time continues to deliver change, and change comes with new challenges—a promise it can surely keep. The region's shift from the past to a time where forward-thinking ideas and inclusivity are essential to the region's heritage reflects a broader effect. The blend of historical roots with contemporary change has created a dynamic region that bridges tradition and progression. No longer are we bound to the ways of our ancestors— rather, we celebrate the opportunities we have to write a different story for ourselves with the many voices that reside here. This work is ongoing.

COMMUNITY CARE

Like the sturdy apple tree that bears fruit each autumn, the fruits of our labor grow with each passing season, nourishing both our spirits and our broader community. The work of a folk practitioner is deeply rooted in service to others. We don't just tend to our altars, gardens, spirits, or work-ings for ourselves; every action to fill our cups allows for the work of nour-ishing those around us too. As a friend and fellow practitioner would say, "You can't pour from an empty cup." In difficult times, we have each other's back, and that's evident in Appalachia.

The long lists of historical folk practitioners prove they were vital figures in their communities. They offered their services with the intent to put their work to good use. They were more than just practitioners; they were pillars of support, embodying the deep interconnectedness that defines community life. Healing in those times went beyond rituals. It was about nurturing kin and ensuring that others felt supported and cared for when they were most vulnerable. Take a young woman in need of postpar-tum care. The local grannies would ensure she had everything she needed to heal as well as support for the newborn child and any other children she may have had. Or perhaps a neighbor who was handling an unfair, messy court case needed justice on their side. The practitioner would craft them a charm bag to carry for the duration of the case. People turned to them to restore balance and offer guidance on crucial matters.

We continue these traditions today thanks to the rise of the internet. Our ancestors would have never imagined how much information we'd have access to—for better or worse. The popularization of witchcraft and other spiritual practices in recent decades parallels internet access in most households, offering a digital space to converse with other practitioners from across the region. Just as local communities historically turned to practitioners in times of need, today's online spaces serve a similar purpose for those limited to physical, safe communities. The internet has facilitated the access of sharing unique personal gnosis, exchanging information, and even educating one another. The accessibility of these online spaces has its pros and cons, but for the most part it offers an opportunity for connecting with like-minded folks and organizing in-person gatherings.

In my own practice, community care is a blend of advocacy and nourishment. My advocacy work includes local causes that are close to my heart, such as affordable housing. My lore of experiencing unstable housing drives my commitment to community involvement. As I write this, there is a dire need nationally for more affordable housing options. The crisis is multifaceted, with rising housing costs, stagnant wages, and a shortage of affordable housing options. This creates an obstacle for achieving the safety and security that comes with having a roof over one's head. The person's well-being is threatened, creating a barrier directing their energy to other facets of their lives. My heart beats fiercely for this since I've experienced similar hardship before, which only inspires me to channel that energy into supporting housing organizations.

Another facet of how I approach community care is rooted in personal and emotional support for others. I recognize my ability to offer a specific kind of tenderness and intuitive support. Perhaps the prominent astrological energy of the Moon within my birth chart guides this work. It is humbling to be someone others trust for a safe space to express themselves or seek divine counsel. I conduct my work with a focus on privacy and sacredness behind closed doors to honor the spiritual nature of the support offered. Reflecting on how my practice and community care intersect, it feels less like a coincidence and more like a natural extension of my path.

This personal desire to support my community within my means goes deeper. In the unearthing of recorded southern Appalachian folk beliefs, I've found a common thread that connects it all that resonates within me: their enduring bond with nature, the ultimate neighbor. A naturally occurring deep connection to personal backyards and mountaintops. This mountain animism permeates every aspect of folklore, where everything is revered as alive and interconnected. It was not only about being a steward of the land, but also being in communion with consented plant folk. The woods have become my own kind of church. Trees have become my teachers. The waters have become my healers.

The notion of community extends beyond our physical neighbors and into the land around us. Through conducting rituals of gratitude, living in alignment with the seasonal shifts, and building reciprocated relationships with the spirits, we are gifted with a safe space to explore ourselves and our work within a relationship that recognizes no hierarchy, but care and collaboration. Engaging with the land in a meaningful way may look like planting a devotional garden with native plants, foraging with intention and gratitude, supporting local conservation efforts, and making more sustainable choices in our everyday lives to combat climate change. Building local connections with the land, the local flora and fauna, only strengthens this rounded concept of community care as we learn so much from this relationship as animists and practitioners.

Honoring the Elders

Honoring our elders from this region includes connecting to their resilient spirit. Not only connecting with our family members of blood and bone but also by place and time. Every family tree is unique in that not everyone has every branch connected to whom they'd consider kin. A family goes beyond just blood relatives and extends to those who have shown up for us. We acknowledge the influential lives of those who made an impact on ourselves and the broader southern mountain region.

The approach of venerating our ancestral spirits is personal and unique to each practitioner. Much of what we know today wouldn't be possible without them instilling some of their wisdom in books or by example. We often look back fondly on our past relatives and preserve some of their traditions in our present homes and with our families. It sparks an inspiration to continue nurturing this relationship even from afar by reading their stories, learning their names, devoting an altar, and invoking their spirit as a helping hand in our work.

While we have learned many of their ways, we've also adopted some of their struggles and pains. The lives of my ancestors—farmers and coal miners and nurses—have all inherently influenced my outlook on life. Their experiences with hard labor and the fear of not making ends meet have instilled a scarcity mindset within me. A persistent fear of not having enough. This mindset has driven a relentless work ethic, often pushing me to overwork myself in a bid to avoid the possibility of losing everything. In a capitalist society that glorifies the grind and constant productivity that equate success with overwork, this inherited mindset can be especially challenging.

As an act of ancestral healing, I have redefined what the "American Dream" means to me. This is an idea that many generations before me were promised. If you work hard, you will be rewarded. You will have a fair chance at living a good life. This was the narrative that inspired many of them to take the leap of faith, only to face a new series of challenges. I find myself experiencing a sense of anger, and have incorporated practices that help unwire the internal response to participate in the hamster wheel of constant productivity. Despite the external pressures, embracing rest and balance becomes a revolutionary act. It is a way to honor my elders. In valuing my well-being over relentless striving, I define what success looks like on my own terms. Success does not mean to suffer. Asking for help does not mean failure. By acknowledging their struggles and choosing a path of balance, I am healing the past and creating a new narrative.

The lessons I've learned from my elders—those of blood and bone, and of place and time—are hard to condense into a single book. It's real, and it's personal. Their guidance has steered me at the big crossroads in life, sending me down paths that have been both challenging and unexpectedly rewarding. Engaging in this ancestral work feels like peeling back layers of myself I didn't even know were there. It's like letting them know that just because they are not of this earth, that they are not forgotten. This work opens the door to mending old wounds and unraveling patterns passed down through generations in a region historically left behind. It's a journey that changes how you see yourself and your place in the world.

While honoring the dead is a big piece of venerating elders, another is remembering that the alive are just as valuable. The stories that are shared over coffee and tea are slowly slipping away. Many of them have yet to be captured. I've made it an active offering for my own ancestors who have passed to go out and seek those stories. To be like the folklorists who recorded so much of what modern folk practitioners use as resources for their magic today. You won't find that many elders will answer to queries about witchcraft, but other subjects that have dual purposes are better received. Ask them about superstitions. Ask them about ghosts or hauntings. Ask them about their parents, and how they would cure wounds. Ask them what they did before dinner or how they prepared for bed. Ask them about the odd things their grandparents did. Or about the meals they cooked on special occasions. This is where folk magic lives. Buried in memories of our past. It is well covered, but easily revealed when the right questions are asked.

Storytelling is one of our oldest traditions. It is woven into our human existence, connecting past to present, preserving knowledge and history, speaking of both light and the dark. Without these stories, we run the risk of severing the threads that tie us to those who came before.

Spending time with our present-day elders can have a profound impact on us as practitioners. You never know whose story is waiting to be heard, seen, and recorded. Storytelling is not meant to be a thing of the past. It is the string that ties me to you, and you to another. The folks within the southern Appalachian region are still very present. We're growing, changing, and showing up more now than ever before with pride. Some keepers of stories are just that—keepers. They may not be willing to open up at first, but some are waiting patiently for a story weaver to join them on the front porch for a good chat. Perhaps that story weaver—the one who recognizes the value in capturing things before they are lost, the one who walks between the liminal space of past and present—is you.

EPILOGUE

From my heart to yours, I hope my delivery can be a guiding lantern. The purpose of this book was not only to continue the conversation of these healing traditions, folkways, and magic, but also to provide a glimpse into southern Appalachia's history by exploring the context of the ever-growing diverse culture. To dig into the depths of the *why* and *how*. From the nourishing farmlands to the comfort of homes to the food served on our plates, it is all a piece of the quilt we wear on our shoulders as *Appalachia*.

I didn't think I'd ever write a book that would be so close to home. Or, rather, one that is about *home* at all. The process of writing this book requested a lot from me, and I was happy to answer the call. It required dedication and emotional investment stored deep in my bones. I'd be lying if I said there were no moments when I experienced a heavy weight on my shoulders with the fear that I'd miss the mark on my intention. This place has historically been left out in the dust and often overlooked. The last thing I wanted was to do the region and the people—my neighbors and friends—a disservice. In surfacing what I wanted to convey, I had to dive into the deeper wells of my own family stories and reignite conversations with fellow practitioners and neighbors. I contacted relatives I hadn't spoken with before and recorded stories from locals to preserve what may become a piece of the past. All in the name of shining more light on these mountains.

Folk magic is not an obvious, in-your-face practice. It is interwoven so intricately that unless you've got your eyes peeled, you might miss it. It is just how things are. It is what it is, as they say. I had a friend who recently expressed how badly she wished she knew of some local folk magic here in the Pacific Northwest. Then, she shared a story that her grandfather told her about a local cryptid. "Sometimes he'd just tell us things to pull our leg," she remarked. I hollered, "But that is where the magic lives!" Stories are central to our folk practices. Without them or the people passing them along, traditions are subject to being forgotten or completely lost.

If you're walking a similar path as myself, let this be whatever voice you need that affirms you're Appalachian enough to be part of this tradition. My family didn't come from a long line of conjurers or healers like other practitioners have described to be their mentors. Not that I am aware of, anyway. Who knows what may be revealed in my family stories after this book is concluded? All I know is that they said their prayers over dinner and told stories after Papaw was done playing his guitar. Sometimes I feel robbed of what could have been if life had turned out a bit differently. Instead, I was taught by other teachers. The neighbors who showed me various folk healing methods and took me on long hikes in the mountains have left a lasting imprint on my work. Just like the time spent with the river spirits, the dogwoods, and the blackberry patches on top of mountains. These are teachers ready to welcome you with open arms.

As I consider this great region from afar, I still carry grievances about leaving my hometown. Some days, I will sit and return in my mind to the apple orchards, my favorite hiking trails, and the Blue Ridge Parkway to feel that comfort again. If I've learned anything from moving away, it's that no matter my whereabouts, some things are deeply engraved in me. Say your prayers before bed. Be sure to call on birthdays. Mind your manners. Sharing is caring. Scratch the left hand for money. This is what I lovingly hold on to. I will stand with my weight against a tall tree and whistle a melody that reminds me of the rolling hills. This is how I return home.

REFERENCES

Ahrens, Kami, ed. *The Foxfire Book of Appalachian Women*. Foxfire Fund, Inc., 2023.

Allen, William Francis, Charles Pickard Ware, and Lucy McKim Garrison, eds. *Slave Songs of the United States*. Dover Publications, 1995.

"Appalachia Then and Now: Examining Changes to the Appalachian Region Since 1965." Appalachian Regional Commission, February 2015. *arc.gov*.

Armstrong, Edward Allworthy. *The Folklore of Birds: An Enquiry into the Origin and Distribution of Some Magico-Religious Traditions*. Houghton Mifflin, 1959.

Ashe, W. W., and H. B. Ayres. *Trees of the Southern Appalachians*. US Forest Service, 1905.

Bardwell, Genevieve, and Susan Ray Brown. *Salt Rising Bread: Recipes and Heartfelt Stories of a Nearly Lost Appalachian Tradition*. St. Lynn's Press, 2016.

Bird, Stephanie Rose. *The Healing Power of African American Spirituality: A Celebration of Ancestor Worship, Herbs and Hoodoo, Ritual and Conjure*. Hampton Roads, 2022.

Boyle, Virginia Frazer. *Devil Tales*. Harper & Brothers, 1900.

Brackman, Barbara. *Barbara Brackman's Civil War Sampler: 50 Quilt Blocks with Stories from History*. C&T Publishing, 2013.

Campbell, John C. *The Southern Highlander and His Homeland*. University Press of Kentucky, 2004.

Carmichael, Alexander. *Carmina Gaedilica: Hymns and Incantations.* Floris Books, 2020.

Casas, Starr. *Old Style Conjure: Hoodoo, Rootwork, and Folk Magic.* Weiser, 2017.

Cavender, A. "Folk Hematology in the Appalachian South." *Journal of Folklore Research* 29, no. 1 (1992): 23–36.

Cavender, A. P. *Folk Medicine in Southern Appalachia.* University of North Carolina Press, 1991.

Chase, Richard. *American Folk Tales and Songs.* Dover Publications, 1971.

Chase, Richard. *The Jack Tales: Folk Tales from the Southern Appalachians.* Houghton Mifflin Company, 1943.

Cheung, Theresa. *The Dream Dictionary from A to Z: The Ultimate A–Z to Interpret the Secrets of Your Dreams.* Harper Element, 2006.

Chiltoskey, Mary Ulmer. *Aunt Mary, Tell Me a Story: A Collection of Cherokee Legends and Tales.* Cherokee Communications, 1990.

Cofield, S. R. "Keeping a Crooked Sixpence: Coin Magic and Religion in the Colonial Chesapeake." *Historical Archaeology* 48, no. 3 (2014): 84–105.

Covey, Herbert C. *African American Slave Medicine: Herbal and Non-Herbal Treatments.* Lexington Books, 2008.

Cross, Tom Peete. "Witchcraft in North Carolina." *Studies in Philology* 16, no. 3 (1919): 217–287.

Cullen, Karen J. *Famine in Scotland: The "Ill Years" of the 1690s.* Edinburgh University Press, 2010.

Dabney, Joseph. *Smokehouse Ham, Spoon Bread and Scuppernong Wine: The Folklore and Art of Southern Appalachian Cooking.* Cumberland House, 2010.

Donmoyer, Patrick J. *Powwowing in Pennsylvania: Braucherei and the Ritual of Everyday Life.* Pennsylvania German Cultural Heritage Center, 2018.

Dunaway, Wilma A. *The First American Frontier: Transition to Capitalism in Southern Appalachia, 1700–1860.* University of North Carolina Press, 1989.

Eden, Sylvia, and Tristan Eden. *Occult Needlecraft.* Leodrune, 2022.

Ehle, John. *Trail of Tears: The Rise and Fall of the Cherokee Nation.* Anchor Books/Doubleday, 1988.

Farr, T. J. "Riddles and Superstitions of Middle Tennessee." *Journal of American Folklore* 48, no. 190 (1935): 318–336.

Fett, Sharla M. *Working Cures: Healing, Health, and Power on Southern Slave Plantations.* University of North Carolina Press, 2002.

The Foxfire Series, 2nd ed. Anchor Books, 1973.

Gainer, Patrick W. *Witches, Ghosts, and Signs: Folklore of the Southern Appalachians.* Vandalia Press, 2008.

Garrett, J. T. *The Cherokee Herbal: Native Plant Medicine from the Four Directions.* Bear & Company, 2003.

Gary, Gemma. *The Black Toad: West Country Witchcraft and Magic.* Troy Books, 2020.

Gary, Gemma. *The Charmers' Psalter.* Troy Books, 2017.

Gladden, Texas. "The Devil's Nine Questions." Recorded by Alan Lomax. *Library of Congress LP AFS L1 Anglo-American Ballads* (volume one), 1942. loc.gov.

Green, E. C. "A Modern Appalachian Folk Healer." *Appalachian Journal* 6, no. 1 (1978): 2–15.

Green, James. *The Devil Is Here in These Hills: West Virginia's Coal Miners and Their Battle for Freedom.* Atlantic Monthly Press, 2015.

Grieve, Margaret. *A Modern Herbal, Volume I.* Dover Publications, 1971.

Gunn, John C. *Gunn's Domestic Medicine, or Poor Man's Friend.* C.M. Saxton, Barker & Company, 1860.

Haizlett, Clara. "Ginseng: The Man-Root That Has Shaped Mankind." Smithsonian Folklife Festival blog, January 29, 2020. *festival.si.edu.*

Hanna, Isaac. "The Company Store." *United Mine Workers Journal,* May 23, 1895. *protestsonglyrics.net.*

Harden, John. *The Devil's Tramping Ground and Other North Carolina Mystery Stories.* University of North Carolina Press, 1980.

Harris, Jessica B. *High on the Hog: A Culinary Journey from Africa to America.* Bloomsbury, 2012.

Herrick, R. F. "The Black Dog of the Blue Ridge." *Journal of American Folklore* 20, no. 77 (1907): 151–152. *doi.org/10.2307/534661.*

Hohman, John George. *The Long-Lost Friend: A 19th Century American Grimoire.* Edited by Daniel Harms. Llewellyn Publications, 2012.

Hudgins, Phil. *The Foxfire Series: Travels with Foxfire: Stories of People, Passions, and Practices from Southern Appalachia.* Anchor Books, 2018.

Hutcheson, Cory Thomas. *Fifty-Four Devils: The Art and Folklore of Fortune-Telling with Playing Cards.* Cory Thomas Hutcheson, 2013.

Hutton, Luke. *The Discovery of a London Monster, Called, The Blacke Dogg of New-gate Profitable for All Readers to Take Heed By.* M[armaduke] P[arsons] for Robert Wilson, at his shop at Grayes-Inne Gate in Holborne, 1638.

Hutton, Ronald. *The Triumph of the Moon.* Oxford University Press, 2021.

Joslin, Michael. *Highland Handcrafters: Appalachian Craftspeople.* Parkway Publishers, 2005.

Kephart, Horace. *Our Southern Highlanders: A Narrative of Adventure in the Southern Appalachians and a Study of Life among the Mountaineers.* University of Tennessee Press, 1976.

Kimmerer, Robin Wall. *Braiding Sweetgrass: Indigenous Wisdom, Scientific Knowledge, and the Teachings of Plants.* Milkweed Editions, 2015.

Lee, Michele Elizabeth. *Working the Roots: Over 400 Years of Traditional African American Healing.* Wadastick, 2017.

Mac Coitir, Niall. *Ireland's Trees: Myths, Legends, and Folklore.* Collins Press, 2016.

Mills, Ash William. *The Black Book of Isobel Gowdie,* 1st ed. Scottish Cunning Ways, 2021.

Mooney, James. "Myths of the Cherokees." *Journal of American Folklore* 1, no. 2 (1888): 97–108.

Mooney, James. "The Cherokee River Cult." *Journal of American Folklore* 13, no. 48 (1900): 1–10.

Mooney, James. *History, Myths, and Sacred Formulas of the Cherokees.* Bright Mountain Books, 1992.

"National Register of Historic Places Inventory—Nomination Form: Zealandia." National Department of the Interior, National Park Service, March 14, 1977.

The Old Farmer's Almanac. Old Farmers Almanac, 2024.

Randolph, Vance. *Ozark Magic and Folklore.* Dover Publications, 1964.

Randolph, Vance. *Ozark Superstitions.* Columbia University Press, 1947.

Reader's Digest Association Limited, London. *Folklore, Myths and Legends of Britain.* F. A. Churchill and Partners, 1977.

Rehder, John B. *Appalachian Folkways.* John Hopkins University Press, 2004.

Rozin, Paul, and Carol Nemeroff. "Sympathetic Magical Thinking: The Contagion and Similarity 'Heuristics.'" In *Heuristics and Biases: The Psychology of Intuitive Judgment,* edited by Thomas Gilovich, Dale Griffin, and Daniel Kahneman. Cambridge University Press, 2002.

Schulke, Daniel A. *The Green Mysteries: Arcana Viridia.* Three Hands Press, 2022.

Skinner, Charles M. "Siren of the French Broad," in *Myths and Legends of Our Own Land.* J. B. Lippincott Company, 1896.

Thomas, Daniel Lindsey, and Lucy Blayney Thomas. *Kentucky Superstitions.* Princeton University Press, 1920.

Tobin, Jacqueline L. *Hidden in Plain View: A Secret Story of Quilts and the Underground Railroad.* Anchor Books, 1999.

Treuer, David. *The Heartbeat of Wounded Knee: Native America from 1890 to the Present.* Riverhead Books, 2019.

Turner, William H. *Blacks in Appalachia.* University of Kentucky Press, 2009.

Velde, Patrick. "Woodwork: Chairs." *Craft Revival: Shaping Western North Carolina Past and Present*, blog, Hunter Library Digital Initiatives and Western Carolina University, accessed December 29, 2024. *wcu.edu.*

Weston, Brandon. *Ozark Folk Magic: Plants, Prayers and Healing.* Llewellyn, 2021.

Whisnant, David E., and Anne Mitchell Whisnant. *Black Lives and Whitened Stories: From the Lowcountry to the Mountains.* National Park Service, 2020.

White, E. G. "Folk-Medicine Among Pennsylvania Germans." *Journal of American Folklore* 10, no. 36 (1897): 78–80.

White, Newman Ivey. *The Frank C. Brown Collection of North Carolina Folklore: Volume 6.* Duke University Press, 1952.

Williams, John Alexander. *Appalachia: A History.* University of North Carolina Press, 2003.

Witthoft, John, and William S. Hadlock. "Cherokee-Iroquois Little People." *Journal of American Folklore* 59, no. 234 (1946): 413–422.

Yarnell, Susan L. "The Southern Appalachians: A History of the Land-scape." United States Department of Agriculture. Forest History Society. www.srs.fs.usda.gov.

Yeats, W. B. *Fairy and Folk Tales of the Irish Peasantry*. W. Scott, 1888.

ABOUT THE AUTHOR

Leah Middleton, also known as The Redheaded Witch in online spaces, is an author and a practitioner of Appalachian folk magic and traditional witchcraft. She shares her practice with those interested in blending magic with the mundane while exploring their ancestral roots, folk practices, and craft. After growing up in western North Carolina, she relocated to the Pacific Northwest in 2022, where she continues to write and owns an online company called Folkcraft Goods.

TO OUR READERS